Mme. Jehane Benoit's Complete Heritage of Canadian Cooking

Mme. Jehane Benoit's Complete Heritage of Canadian Cooking

PAGURIAN PRESS LIMITED

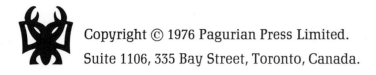

DISTRIBUTED IN CANADA BY

JOHN WILEY & SONS CANADA LIMITED

22 Worcester Road
Rexdale, Ontario

ISBN 0-88932-040-3

Printed and bound in the United States of America

Contents

Introduction

"My life is good food, lovingly prepared." With this simple statement, Mme. Jehane Benoit describes the credo which has elevated her to the foremost ranks as an interpreter of French, Canadian, and other cooking styles from around the world. Mme. Benoit has been feted in North America for her innovations, her dedication, her brilliance in putting forward a simple and consistently pleasurable style of cuisine.

In private life, Mme. Benoit lives on her sheep farm in the rolling, peaceful countryside of the Eastern Townships, 75 miles southeast of Montreal. Here, in her comfortable farm kitchen, she creates her recipes — testing them, changing, improving, adding, until she is satisfied with the result. In addition to striving for culinary perfection, Mme. Benoit also studies the history of a recipe, discovering its source, its antecedents, its development over the years. Her skill is honed not only by the scholarship of her training, but the practical cauldron of regular entertaining.

This book is a labor of love for Mme. Benoit, for it contains her very own favorite recipes, the ones she uses most in the busy round of entertaining, the ones she chooses for her own guests. Here is an inside look at the secrets and special favorites of a woman who has become the cooking advisor to a nation.

From her vast kaleidoscope of experience, Mme. Benoit has chosen the recipes which reflect her belief in Escoffier's teachings, summed up in the phrase: "Make it simple."

Mme. Benoit makes it simple . . . and good.

Bon appetit!

Appetizers

Terrine de Campagne

A terrine is a meat loaf with personality. A slice of this pâté, with crusty French bread and a glass of light red wine, is indeed an elegant hors d'oeuvre.

 1 lb. lamb or pork liver
 1 cup chopped onions
 2 garlic cloves, crushed
 ¼ cup brandy
 ⅔ cup port wine
 ¼ lb. each, ground veal and pork
 1½ tsp. salt
 ½ tsp. pepper
 1 bay leaf
 1 tsp. each, tarragon and thyme
 2 eggs, beaten
   strips of side bacon

Coarsely chop the liver with a sharp knife (do not grind it) and place in a non-metal bowl with the onion, garlic, brandy, and port. Cover and refrigerate for 24 hours to marinate.

Add remaining ingredients except bacon and mix thoroughly (an electric mixer can be used at medium speed for 5 minutes).

Line a terrine or an 8 x 5 inch loaf pan with strips of bacon. Pour in the meat mixture, place in a pan of hot water, and bake, uncovered, in a 350°F. oven for 1 hour. Turn heat down to 300°F. and bake 30 minutes more.

Remove from oven, cover with foil or wax paper, and put a heavy object on top — the chefs use a brick, but a can of tomatoes or something similar will do. Refrigerate for 12 hours; unmold. A terrine will keep for 2 to 3 weeks refrigerated; 2 months frozen. Serves 12.

Variations: Replace veal and pork with an equal amount of raw wild or domestic duck. Or, when marinating the liver, add ½ lb. of coarsely chopped venison, sliced raw pheasant, or partridge breasts. Make terrine, layering thin slices of pheasant or partridge between liver mixture. The baking time remains the same.

Caviar Mousse

This mousse is sister Jacqueline's creation — easy, quick to make, and a showpiece at cocktail time. Do not worry about the pie plate mold; once decorated, it looks very elegant.

 1 envelope unflavored gelatine
 2 tbsp. cold water
 ½ cup boiling water
 2 tbsp. mayonnaise (not sweet dressing)
 ¼ tsp. dry mustard
 1 tbsp. tarragon or red wine vinegar
 1 tbsp. Worcestershire sauce
 1 jar (3½ oz.) Danish lumpfish caviar (black)
 1 loaf black bread

Soak the gelatine in the cold water for 5 minutes. Add the boiling water and stir over low heat until gelatine has dissolved.

Remove from heat and add the mayonnaise, dry mustard, vinegar, Worcestershire sauce, and caviar. Stir until well mixed.

Oil a 9-inch Corning pie plate. Pour in the mixture, cover with plastic wrap, and refrigerate overnight.

To serve, slide a knife around the edges of the plate; unmold on a round, flat, 10-to-12-inch plate. My sister uses a silver tray or a cut glass ice cream plate — I prefer the cut glass.

Surround with fingers of thinly sliced, buttered black bread, along with napkins and small knives. Guests can then help themselves to the bread, spreading it with the caviar mousse.

Dainty Beef Rolls

These finger-sized rolls should be served hot with a half-and-half mixture of Dijon mustard and chili sauce, and small fingers of crustless rye bread.

   ½ lb. ground round
   1 medium onion, grated
   2 eggs
   2 tsp. curry powder
   ½ tsp. cumin seeds
   4 tbsp. fine, dry bread crumbs
   ½ cup chopped fresh parsley
   1 tsp. salt
   salad oil

Place all ingredients except the oil in a bowl. Mix and knead until very smooth (or beat at medium speed in an electric mixer for 5 minutes). It must be worked until mixture is a smooth paste.

Wet your hands, take a small piece of mixture and roll between your palms into the shape of a little finger. Set on wax paper until all the paste has been rolled. Refrigerate until needed.

Heat oil in a frying pan over high heat. When hot, reduce heat to medium or place pan on another burner at medium heat; add a few meat fingers at a time (do not crowd them), and fry until golden, about 3 to 4 minutes each. Serves 8 to 10.

Mushroom Rolls

These are served hot, two rolls per person, with crisp, cold celery sticks. Prepare rolls ahead of time and keep refrigerated.

   12 thin slices white bread
      soft butter
   ½ lb. finely chopped fresh mushrooms
   4 tbsp. butter
   ½ tsp. curry powder
   1 tbsp. lemon juice
   ½ tsp. salt
   ¼ tsp. pepper

Remove crusts from bread and roll slices with a rolling pin to make them even thinner. Spread with soft butter and set aside.

Melt 2 tbsp. of butter with curry and lemon juice. Add mushrooms and sauté over high heat for 3 minutes, stirring constantly. Sprinkle with the salt and pepper.

Spread about 1 tbsp. of mushrooms over each slice of bread. Roll jelly-roll fashion; fasten each roll with picks and place on a baking sheet. Melt last 2 tbsp. of butter, brush it lightly over rolls, and refrigerate. When ready to serve, bake rolls in a 425°F. oven for about 15 minutes, or until light brown. Serves 6.

Liptauer Cheese

An Austrian delicacy, this recipe was given to me by a Viennese ballet dancer. Liptauer Cheese has been a part of my cooking repertoire for many years.

   1 4 oz. pkg. cream cheese
   2 tbsp. cream
   1 tbsp. paprika
   1 tsp. caraway seeds
   1 tsp. capers
   1 tbsp. chives

Blend all the ingredients thoroughly. Serve with black bread. Serves 4 to 6.

Cheddar Cheese Wafers

These crisp cheese wafers are easy to prepare and, if stored in a metal box in a cool place, will keep for months. Serve them hot or cold.

   1 cup grated, strong cheddar cheese
   1 cup crushed potato chips
   ¼ cup soft butter
   ½ cup all-purpose flour
   1 tsp. prepared mustard

Measure the cheese and potato chips (after grating and crushing). Put the mixture in a bowl, add the remaining ingredients, and blend. Place on an unbuttered baking sheet in small spoonfuls, flattening slightly with the bottom of the spoon.

Bake at 375°F. for 5 to 8 minutes, or until golden brown, then cool on a cake rack. To serve hot, reheat at 300°F. for a few minutes.

Blue Cheese Roll

This most delicious cheese mixture will keep well for 3 to 4 weeks; hence it is useful as an appetizer when unexpected guests drop in.

  ½ lb. Roquefort or Danish blue cheese
   8 oz. pkg. cream cheese
   3 tbsp. soft butter
   3 tbsp. brandy
   2 tbsp. minced chives or green onions
     chopped, roasted almonds
     round, unsalted crackers

Mash cheeses with butter, brandy, and green onions or chives. When smooth and creamy, refrigerate for 1 hour. Form mixture into a cylinder 1½ inches in diameter and roll it in the almonds. Wrap well and refrigerate. To serve, cut into thin slices; place each slice on a round cracker. Yield: 2½ to 3 dozen rounds.

Pickled Mushrooms

Each year I pickle 6 to 10 pints of little button mushrooms, as they keep indefinitely under refrigeration and are delicious either as an appetizer, as a condiment with fish or duck, or, as a garnish for vegetables or a rice salad.

   3 lbs. small button mushrooms
     cider vinegar
   1 tsp. salt
     salad oil
   1 tbsp. mixed pickling spice or 1 tbsp. peeled
     fresh ginger, sliced

Rinse the whole, unpeeled mushrooms in a colander under warm, then cold water. Transfer to a saucepan and cover with a mixture of half cider vinegar and half water (measure 1 cup of each, then add as needed). Season with salt and boil for 15 minutes. Drain liquid into another pan; let the mushrooms cool.

Mix 1 cup cider vinegar with 1 cup salad oil and add spices. Fill sterilized jars one-quarter full with the reserved liquid. Add mushrooms and pack them down well. Fill jars (placed on a plate to catch the overflow), to overflowing, with the oil and vinegar mixture. Cover and refrigerate. Makes 2 pints.

Special Sandwich Spread

Special because it has only 9 calories per tablespoon, it can be spread (without butter) on melba toast, Rye-Krisp, whole wheat bread, or, if you can afford 100 calories, on a roll.

   4 medium carrots, scrubbed
  ½ green pepper, finely chopped (optional)
   3 celery stalks, finely chopped
   2 tbsp. chopped walnuts
   2 tbsp. wheat germ
   1 tbsp. prepared horseradish, well drained
   3 tbsp. low-calorie, mayonnaise-type dressing
   1 tbsp. lemon juice
     salt, to taste

Grate the carrots on the finest grater, add remaining ingredients, and stir until well mixed. Refrigerated in a covered glass jar it will keep for 3 days. Yield: 2 cups.

Devilled Almonds

In winter, everyone will love to pick these tasty tidbits right from the pan with their fingers. In the summer they are better served cold.

   4 tbsp. butter
   1 to 1½ cups blanched almonds
   1 tbsp. each, chutney sauce, brown sugar, and
     Worcestershire sauce
  ½ tsp. each, curry powder and turmeric
  ¼ tsp. salt
     pinch of cayenne

Melt the butter in a 300°F. electric frying pan and brown nuts, one layer deep, stirring and tossing them. Combine the remaining ingredients, add to the nuts, and stir until sugar melts. Serves 6 to 8.

Pickled Wild Mushrooms

Pickled wild mushrooms were a contribution of the English settlers. Gathering wild mushrooms is a lost art now, but this old recipe can be made equally well with cultivated mushrooms. They make a most pleasant hors d'oeuvre or pickle.

Tie up in a piece of cheesecloth: several strips of parsley, a pinch of thyme, a bay leaf, a whole clove, and a dozen peppercorns. Put these in a saucepan with 2 cups water, 1 cup olive oil, ½ cup vinegar (I sometimes use lemon juice instead of vinegar). Boil for 5 minutes. Then add 1 lb. button mushrooms, the stems neatly clipped off; boil for 15 minutes more. Remove from heat and discard the spice bag. Let the mushrooms cool in the juice. Pot, seal, and keep in a cool, dark place.

Ham Persillade

A classic recipe from Burgundy in France, and surely the most elegant of all jellied meats.

    5 to 8-lb. ham, boned and rolled
10-oz. can beef consommé, undiluted
½ bottle dry white wine
    2 cups water
    1 meatless veal knuckle bone
½ cup minced fresh parsley
    1 tbsp. tarragon
    2 bay leaves
½ tsp. thyme
    3 small onions, quartered
    1 garlic clove, crushed
¼ tsp. pepper

    2 envelopes unflavored gelatine
¼ cup cold water
    1 cup minced fresh parsley
    2 tbsp. brandy or lemon juice

Place the ham in a saucepan. Add all ingredients except last four. Bring to a boil, reduce heat, cover, and simmer until the ham is tender, 1 to 2 hours. When cooked, remove ham from broth and trim off the rind. Cut the ham and fat into narrow pieces, but do not chop too finely or slice too thinly. Put the cooking juice through a fine sieve and add the gelatine, soaked 5 minutes in the cold water. Stir together until gelatine is completely dissolved, then refrigerate until the fat is sufficiently set on top to be removed.

In the meantime, press the cut ham into a mold or loaf tin. Cover and refrigerate until the broth is ready. Remove the fat and pour 2 cups of the broth over the ham, allowing it to penetrate entirely. Refrigerate again to jell. This will take 30 to 60 minutes.

Mix the last two ingredients into remaining broth, pour over the ham, cover the mold carefully, and refrigerate. Serve, unmolded, with herb mustard.

This jellied ham may be prepared 4 to 6 days in advance. Serve on thinly sliced black bread with drinks before dinner or with a cold white Burgundy for a buffet.

Soups

My Special Chicken Stock

This stock costs little to make, yet it has a distinctive flavor. Serve it as a consommé with a few thin slices of raw mushrooms, or slivers of green onions, or long shreds of raw carrots.

    1 lb. chicken wings or legs
      chicken bones (optional)
    2 green onions, cut into 3 pieces
    3 thick slices fresh ginger root
    2 tsps. salt
    8 cups cold water

Place all the ingredients in saucepan. Bring to a fast boil, then reduce the heat and simmer over low heat, uncovered, for about 1 hour. When necessary, skim the surface. Cool; taste for seasoning. Strain through a fine sieve. Pour in a glass jam jar, cover and refrigerate until needed. Serves 6.

Aberdeen Bouillon

Bouillon contains almost no calories. Starting dinner with a good cup of bouillon not only cuts one's appetite, but makes the whole meal more of a special occasion.

    1 round shoulder beef bone or 1 oxtail (Ask
      your butcher for a bone with some lean meat
      on it.)
    2 carrots, scrubbed and sliced
    1 celery stalk with leaves
    1 onion, diced
    1 bay leaf
    ¼ tsp. thyme
    1 cup canned tomatoes with liquid
    8 cups cold water
    1 tsp. salt
    6 peppercorns

Bring all the ingredients to a boil in a large saucepan; remove scum, if any. Cover, and simmer slowly for 3 hours.

Strain, reserving meat and bone; cool. (The meat from the bone can be used to make a salad.) Pour liquid into quart jars, cover, and refrigerate. When cold, the fat will rise to the top and can be removed; what's left is a delicious, clear, fat-free bouillon. Serve it hot or cold as is, or garnish with minced celery, cucumber, parsley, or green onions. Yield: 8 cups.

Consommé Maharajah

Homemade chicken or beef consommé has the best flavor, but diluted canned consommé can also be used to make this festive soup.

Pour boiling hot consommé into a tureen. Set the tureen on a tray, surround it with bouillon cups, a decanter of sherry, a bowl of grated cheese, herb biscuits, curried rice, and petals of chrysanthemum. Let each guest garnish his consommé according to his taste.

Curried Consommé

Curried consommé is a light, tasty soup best served when chicken, duck, or veal is the main course.

    2 tbsp. butter
    1 large onion, chopped
    2 slices bacon, diced
    1 tbsp. curry powder
    1 tbsp. flour
    6 cups bouillon (stock, canned, or made from
      cubes)
    ⅓ cup uncooked, long grain rice
    ⅓ cup parsley, minced
    ⅓ cup grated cheese

Fry onion and bacon in butter. Season with curry powder and stir until well mixed. Add flour and blend. Add bouillon and rice. Stir well and bring to the boil.

Cover and simmer over low heat for 30 to 40 minutes. Serve in warm bowls, sprinkling each serving with parsley and grated cheese. Serves 6.

Japanese Consommé

Here is another low-calorie starter. It is easy to make, and pleases both the eye and the palate.

Boil together an equal quantity of clam juice and undiluted consommé. To serve, pour into small porcelain cups. Top each serving with a pale pink rose petal.

Leek Base for Vichyssoise

Make this leek base in the autumn when fresh leeks are plentiful and cheap. From it, a gourmet soup can be prepared in 20 minutes, all year around.

    12 medium-sized leeks
     4 large, mild onions
    1½ cups butter

Remove the top coarse leaves from leeks. Cut a long slit from the white part to the end of the green part. Wash carefully under running cold water, shaking off surplus water. Cut into thin slices, starting at the white base. Peel and slice the onions as thinly as possible. Melt the butter in a saucepan, add the leeks and onions; stir well. Cover and cook over very low heat for 25 minutes, stirring a few times. The mixture must soften completely but not brown. (It will diminish in size quite a bit.) Divide by cupfuls into containers and freeze. Yield: 3 pints.

Vichyssoise

Bring 3 to 4 cups chicken consommé to the boil, add 1 cup of the frozen leek mixture. Simmer for 20 minutes. Beat in 1 cup instant mashed potatoes, previously stirred with ½ cup cold milk. Simmer together for a few minutes. Add 1 cup cream. When the soup is creamy, taste for seasoning and serve. Or, the soup can be strained, refrigerated, and served cold.

Cucumber Vichyssoise

This quick soup can be made in a blender. Hot or cold, it is delicious.

    1 can (10½ oz.) frozen cream of potato soup
    ½ cup milk
    1 medium cucumber
    ½ cup heavy cream, or 1 cup commercial sour cream
      minced fresh dill, or paprika, or watercress (for cold soup only), or minced chives (for hot soup)

Partially thaw the can of frozen cream of potato soup and put the chunks in a blender. Cover and blend at high speed. Add milk and cucumber, which has been peeled, seeded, and cut into 2-inch pieces. Cover and blend for a few seconds.

Pour the mixture into a bowl and add heavy cream or sour cream. Taste for seasoning and stir well. Refrigerate until ready to serve.

When serving it cold, simply garnish with dill, paprika, or watercress. To serve hot, heat and garnish with chives. Serves 4.

Cold Cream of Cucumber Soup

This is a famous Polish summer soup. I often serve it with a bowl of boiled shrimps, cooled and mixed with a little French dressing — a light but satisfying meal.

    3 large cucumbers, peeled and thinly sliced
    3 tbsp. butter
    1 cup green beet tops, chopped
    2 green onions, diced
    3 tbsp. flour
      salt and pepper, to taste
    4 cups chicken broth or consommé
    ½ cup rich cream
    1 to 2 tbsp. chives, chopped
    1 tbsp. fresh dill

In a saucepan, melt the butter, add the cucumbers, beet tops, and green onions. Simmer over low heat for 10 minutes, stirring a few times.

Sift the flour over the cucumbers, season to taste with salt and pepper, and mix together until well blended. Add the chicken broth or consommé. Stir until slightly thickened; simmer over low heat for 15 minutes. Pass through a food mill or sieve, or blend in an electric blender. Adjust seasoning.

Refrigerate, covered, until cold. Add the cream, chives, and dill. Serve well chilled. Serves 6.

French Onion Soup

4 to 5 large onions
4 tablespoons butter
2 tablespoons all-purpose flour
6 cups tepid water or consommé
2 cups milk (optional)
1 teaspoon coarse salt
¼ teaspoon pepper
4 to 6 slices toasted bread

Peel the onions and cut in two. Slice each half as thinly and as evenly as possible. Heat the butter in a large heavy skillet. Add the onions and stir almost constantly with a wooden spoon, until the onions are golden brown. Then add the flour and continue cooking over low heat stirring often, until it takes on a light golden color.

Add the water or consommé and the salt. Bring to a boil stirring constantly, and then simmer over low heat from 8 to 10 minutes.

In the meantime, toast the bread. Place one slice in each plate and sprinkle with pepper.

Add the scalded milk to the soup. Taste for seasoning and pour over the bread slices. Serve with a bowl of grated cheese. To serve this soup with Swiss cheese: Slice very thin or grate ½ pound of cheese. Place one-third of the toasted bread slices in the bottom of a soup kettle or a pyrex dish. Sprinkle (or cover) with one-third of the cheese. Make 3 such layers. Pour the onion soup with or without milk over. Cover and place in a 400°F. oven for 10 minutes.

To make *gratinée* onion soup: For a good *gratin* use a dish that is wider than it is high, so that the oven heat is spread over a larger surface. A few minutes before serving, pour the onion soup in the dish. Top with the toasted bread and sprinkle generously with the grated or sliced cheese. Pour 1 tablespoon lightly peppered melted butter over the cheese. Place in a 500°F. oven to obtain a lovely golden crust (from 10 to 20 minutes). Serve immediately.

Ham Persillade, a classic recipe from Burgundy — the most elegant of all jellied meats. Recipe on page 12.

Fish and Shellfish

3

Cornell Oven-Fried Fillets

This new method of frying fish was developed at Cornell University. One gets the same crisp brown crust and flavor of pan-fried fish, yet less fat is used, it requires less attention, and makes almost no odor.

Partially thaw 1 lb. of fish fillets. Stir 1 tsp. of salt into ½ cup of milk. Mix 1 cup of fine, dry bread crumbs and 1 tsp. of paprika. Dip each portion of fish into the milk, then roll in the bread crumbs.

Oil, grease, or butter (bacon fat gives a good flavor) a shallow baking pan and arrange the fillets in it, side by side. Drizzle 2 tbsp. of melted butter over them and bake, uncovered, in a preheated 500°F. oven for 8 to 10 minutes, or until fish flakes when tested with a fork. Serve as is or with tartar sauce. Serves 3.

Broiled Fish Orientale

To become a really good cook you must develop an almost sixth sense as to when something has cooked just enough and is at its peak in flavor and texture. A recipe helps to a degree, but a natural food sense, coupled with experience are of paramount importance. When it comes to fish, the best and only advice is: do not overcook. If the heat is too high or the cooking too long, the fish will be dry and tough and the whole house will smell of it. Remember the rule — ten minutes per inch thickness, regardless of the cooking method.

Water is the secret of the following recipe. High heat is used, but the fish is protected by the humidity of the water.

Fillet of Sole Florentine — a superb combination of sole fillets and a cheese and mushroom sauce, over a bed of lightly cooked spinach. Recipe on page 21.

Place fish fillets (any kind) on an oiled rack set in a shallow broiling pan. Sprinkle (do not roll) the fillets generously with fine bread crumbs, dot with butter, and pour one-quarter inch of hot water in the pan.

Preheat broiler to 550°F. or, for 15 minutes. (This is important.) Set the broiler pan 3 to 4 inches away from the source of heat, and broil for *exactly* 5 minutes, unless you are broiling very thin fillets, which may cook in 3 minutes. (Most fillets are half an inch thick.)

Italian Baked Fillets

Serve with spinach and a tomato salad: a great combination.

2 lbs. frozen fish fillets
1 cup commercial sour cream
½ cup chopped green onions
½ tsp. salt
¼ tsp. pepper
⅓ cup grated Parmesan cheese

Thaw fillets just enough to separate them. Arrange in a well-greased, shallow baking casserole. Combine remaining ingredients and spread evenly over each portion. Bake in a 350°F. oven for 20 to 25 minutes, then sprinkle with paprika. Serves 6.

Broiled Frozen Fillets

To retain the flavor in broiled frozen fillets, start cooking them the moment their outside surface loses its icy rigidity, while they are still a little difficult to separate. Then, if quickly seared under the broiler, they will retain their original flavor and moisture.

Preheat the broiler and grease the broiler pan only where the fish are to go. Do not use a wire rack. Rub fillets first with fresh lemon juice, then brush generously with melted butter, bacon fat, or salad oil.

Arrange them in the broiler pan 2 inches away from source of heat. Without turning fillets, broil them for 8 to 12 minutes or a few minutes more if the fillets were hard-frozen. Serve immediately.

Quick Wine Sauces for Fish

For baked, pan fried, or broiled fish

Heat together (do not boil) an equal mixture of each of the following: butter, dry white wine, fresh lemon juice, grated lemon rind to taste, and fresh minced parsley. Pour over fish or serve separately.

For breaded or deep fried fish, or hot fish sticks

Combine in top half of double boiler or in a small, heavy enamel cast iron saucepan: 1 cup grated strong or medium cheddar cheese, 1 can undiluted cream of celery soup, ¼ cup dry sherry, and 2 tablespoons minced chives or parsley.

Heat over low heat, stirring often until cheese has melted and the sauce is very hot.

Fish Hash

When I have leftover fish and potatoes, I always make this dish and refrigerate or freeze it to have on hand for a quick breakfast or lunch.

> cold, cooked fish fillets (at least 1 cup)
> equal quantity cold, boiled potatoes
> 1 large onion, grated
> ¼ tsp. sage
> 1 egg, beaten
> 3 tbsp. margarine

Flake the fish and cut the potatoes into small pieces. Combine with onion; add sage and beaten egg.

Melt margarine in a large frying pan. When hot, add the fish mixture, press it down, and cook over medium heat until crusty brown underneath. Invert on to a hot platter and sprinkle with minced parsley or green onions, or spread with catsup. (If the hash has been frozen, thaw it first over low heat, then raise heat to medium and continue as outlined.)

Braised Haddock with Savory Balls

This was one of my mother's favorites. A Scottish nanny taught her how to make it, and it is still a very tasty way to serve fish.

Braised Haddock
> 7 slices bacon
> 1½ to 2 lbs. fillets of haddock
> rind of 1 lemon, grated
> ½ tsp. salt
> ¼ tsp. freshly ground pepper

Line a baking dish with 4 slices of bacon. Top with the haddock fillets. Cover with 3 slices of bacon.

Mix the grated lemon rind with the salt and pepper. Sprinkle on top of fish and bacon.

Place the savory balls (see below) around the fish, cover the dish with its cover or a sheet of foil, and bake in a preheated 425°F. oven for 25 minutes. Uncover and bake for 5 minutes more. Serves 6.

Savory Balls
> ⅔ cup well-packed fresh bread crumbs
> 1 tbsp. dried parsley
> ¼ tsp. dried sage or savory
> 1 small onion, minced
> 2 slices bacon, diced
> ½ tsp. salt
> ¼ tsp. pepper
> 2 eggs

Place in a bowl the bread crumbs, dried parsley, dried sage or savory, minced onion, diced bacon, salt, pepper, and eggs.

Mash and blend with your hands until well mixed. Shape into small balls.

Broil-Poached Haddock

Fish is first on the list in any figure-conscious diet, so why not serve it once a week? The following method is perfect because the oils cook out of the fish, yet it retains a rich treasure trove of iodine and minerals.

Staying with the diet idea, start the meal with a large bowl of icy cold, crisp celery, radishes, carrot sticks, green onions, and a few olives.

> 4 1-inch-thick haddock fillets or steaks
> 1 cup hot water
> 2 tbsp. fresh lemon juice
> 1 tsp. salt
> ½ tsp. pepper
> 3 tbsp. melted butter
> ¼ tsp. curry powder
> 1 minced green onion
> lemon sections
> chopped fresh parsley

Arrange individual portions of fish in a shallow baking dish. Mix the water with the lemon juice, salt, and pepper. Pour this mixture over the fish. Then place the fish under the broiler, about 4 inches from the heat. When the water boils, broil 7 to 8 minutes more. The top should be brown and the fillets opaque and easily flaked when touched with a fork. The water will be coated with oil. Lift the fish out carefully with a wide-slotted spatula on to a hot platter. Keep warm.

Melt the butter with the curry powder and green onion. Pour over fish and serve immediately. Garnish with lemon sections and sprinkle with parsley. Serves 4.

Fillet of Sole Florentine

This colorful dish is perfect to serve to lunch or supper guests.

> 1 lb. fresh spinach
> ¼ tsp. sugar
> butter, flour, light cream and milk (see instructions)
> pinch of nutmeg
> 4 to 6 small sole fillets
> ½ cup thinly sliced fresh mushrooms
> ½ cup grated cheese
> 2 tbsp. chopped parsley

Wash spinach and pack into a saucepan without water — what clings to the leaves is sufficient. Sprinkle with sugar, cover, and cook over medium heat four minutes; then turn over so top leaves will be on the bottom and cook another two minutes. Remove from heat but do not drain.

Cream spinach in the following manner: place 1 tbsp. butter on top, sprinkle with 2 tbsp. flour, add 2 tbsp. light cream and the nutmeg and stir together. Season to taste. Spread evenly in a well-buttered 1½-quart baking dish and cover with fillets, either left flat or rolled.

Quickly fry mushrooms in 2 tbsp. butter for 2 to 3 minutes only. Do not season. Spread over fillets.

Make a white sauce with 2 tbsp. butter, ¼ cup flour and ½ cup each light cream and milk. Add cheese, parsley, and salt and pepper to taste. Pour sauce over fish; bake 30 minutes in a 375°F. oven. Serves 6.

Barbecued Shrimps

A 7-pound box of frozen, uncooked shrimps (purchased from a wholesale fish dealer) makes an exciting barbecue for ten, at less cost than steak. Try it.

> 2 to 3 lbs. uncooked shrimps
> ⅓ cup olive oil
> ⅓ cup plus 1 tsp. lemon juice
> 1½ tsp. curry powder
> 1 tsp. crushed garlic or ½ tsp. garlic powder
> 1 tsp. salt
> 1 cup chutney
> 2 tbsp. brandy
> hot bread

Rinse shrimps in cold water. If they are frozen, let them soak for 30 minutes — they will then be easy to separate. Shell and devein.

Stir together olive oil, ⅓ cup lemon juice, curry powder, garlic or garlic powder, and salt.

Add the shelled shrimps to the mixture and stir until well blended. Cover and refrigerate for 3 to 6 hours, stirring once or twice. Then remove shrimps from marinade. Strain and reserve the liquid.

Adjust the grill 3 inches from hot coals. Place shrimps on the grill and cook for 5 minutes without turning, basting several times with the marinade.

Mix chutney with the remaining 1 teaspoon lemon juice and brandy. Use this as a dip. Serve grilled shrimps with the dip and plenty of hot bread. Serves 4 to 6.

Shrimps Superba

Do not attempt to make this recipe with frozen or canned shrimps. Large, uncooked shrimps are a must. Cooked on the hibachi or in an electric frying pan in front of your guests, followed by a tray of assorted cheeses, crisp crackers, home-made breads, and a bottle of white wine, here is a delectable, do-it-yourself lunch.

1½ lbs. fresh shrimps, unshelled
    juice and grated rind from 2 limes
2 tsp. coarse salt
3 to 6 tbsp. salad oil
3 limes, quartered

Split the shrimps in half lengthwise through the shell and tail. Rinse out dark vein. Dry shrimps on paper towels; arrange on platter, cut side up; dribble with the lime juice and sprinkle with grated rind and salt. Cover with waxed paper and refrigerate for 3 to 6 hours.

To serve, heat the oil in large frying pan. Working with half the shrimps at a time, skin side down, sauté until shells are pink, about 2 minutes per side, turning only once. Transfer to a warm platter surrounding it with the quartered limes, for everyone to use according to taste. Serves 4.

Take a Can of Seafood — et, Voila!

Great eating can be had from canned seafood. When you find how versatile salmon, tuna, bonito, lobster, crab, shrimp, oysters, and all the other ready-cooked fish can be, you will use them more and more. Here are a few of my favorite quick seafood dishes.

Quick Seafood Casserole
Take any canned seafood — lobster, crab, shrimp, oysters — and arrange in a flat baking dish. Add ¼ cup sherry, a sprinkling of tarragon, 2 tbsp. butter cut into small pieces, and ¼ cup table cream or ½ cup sour cream. Cover with My Favorite Crumb Topping and bake 10 minutes at 300°F.

My Favorite Crumb Topping: Combine ¼ cup crushed crackers, ¼ tsp. paprika, 2 tbsp. melted butter or olive oil, 1 tbsp. crushed potato chips, 2 tsp. grated Parmesan cheese, and a pinch of tarragon or thyme.

Fish Pie
Line a pie plate with ready-mixed pastry. Break up the contents of any 7-oz. can of fish or seafood. Add to it 1 cup milk, ½ cup fine soft bread crumbs, 2 beaten eggs, ½ tsp. curry or dill seeds, a finely chopped onion, salt, pepper, and parsley (if you like it). Place this mixture in the crust-lined plate. (Flute the edges nicely.)

Now you have your choice of four finishing touches — either leave it as it is, or, top with a crust, or sprinkle the top with ½ cup grated cheese or ½ cup sour cream beaten into an egg with a dash of nutmeg. No matter which recipe you choose, the pie bakes 30 to 35 minutes at 375°F. The texture is creamy; the flavor, delicious.

Fish Pie — The Quebec Way
Line a pie plate with ready-mixed pastry. Fill it with mashed potatoes flavored with savory and chopped green onions. Top with a 7-oz. can of salmon or 2 cans of sardines. Cover with a crust, and bake until golden brown at 375°F. This makes a good supper.

No Meat, and No Hurry: Make a potato pie. Line pie plate with your favorite packaged pie crust. Make mashed potatoes with those wonderful instant flaked potatoes. Instead of butter, add ½ cup sour cream to potatoes when ready. Place in bottom of crust, top with 1 cup cottage cheese or 1 can salmon. Top with ½ cup sour cream, 1 egg, and minced onion to taste, blended together. Then top with pie crust. Bake in 400°F. oven until golden brown. Good hot or cold. Serve with assorted pickles.

Sardines à la Basque
Heat 1 or 2 cans of sardines in their own oil. Then drain and arrange them on toast. Toast and sardines are served with small boiled potatoes that have been covered with white sauce or a warmed-up can of undiluted celery soup, then sprinkled with minced parsley, chives, or chopped hard-boiled egg.

Sardine Roll Niçoise

Split and lightly butter long, crisp rolls. On one half arrange thin slices of tomato and shreds of green pepper or onion rings. On the other half spread 2 or 3 mashed sardines, well seasoned with lemon juice, chopped parsley, or garlic. Press the two halves together and serve with a salad.

Fish Casserole Florentine

Boil half of an 8-oz. package of spaghetti. Drain, mix 1 tbsp. butter, and arrange in a casserole. Over it spread 2 cups chopped well-drained and seasoned canned spinach. Cover the spinach with the contents of a can of any coarse-flaked fish. Top all with 2 cups white sauce made from 2 tbsp. butter, 2 tbsp. flour, 1 cup milk, and the reserved juice drained from the spinach (adding milk if there is less than a cup of spinach liquid). Season with salt and pepper, and, when the sauce has cooked, add 1 tsp. lemon juice, 1 tbsp. mayonnaise, and a pinch of dill. Sprinkle the casserole with ½ cup grated cheese and bake 30 minutes at 350°F. This dish is good the whole year around and is sure to become a great favorite of your family and guests.

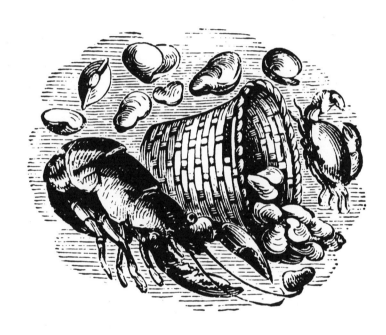

Poultry

4

Crisp Steam-Baked Chicken

Serve with a green salad, or, with celery and carrot sticks — only 175 calories per serving (not counting the gravy)!

> **3-lb. broiler**
> **½ tsp. salt**
> **pinch of garlic powder**
> **½ tsp. tarragon or basil**
> **¼ tsp. pepper**
> **paprika**

Quarter the chicken and put it in a shallow baking dish, skin side up. Mix all ingredients except paprika and sprinkle over the pieces. Sprinkle generously with paprika. Cover, using foil if necessary, and bake in a 350°F. oven for 1½ hours, or until golden. Serves 4.

My Favorite Broiled Chicken

You will find that this dish is good served cold, but even better if it has not been refrigerated.

> **2½ to 3 lb. broiler**
> **salt and pepper**
> **3 tbsp. salad oil**
> **1 tsp. paprika**
> **½ tsp. crumbled dried tarragon, basil, savory or ¼ tsp. ground thyme or sage**

Separate the chicken into halves with poultry shears or a pair of good kitchen scissors. It is easy — start by cutting down the back first, then turn and cut through the breastbone. Remove the backbone and the neck and use these for making stock. Twist the wing joints in their sockets so the pieces will lie flat.

Place the bird, skin side down, directly on the broiler pan, not on a rack. Sprinkle the top with salt and pepper, pour the salad oil on top, and sprinkle with paprika. Sprinkle the herb of your choice over the pieces.

Place the broiler pan in the lowest part of a preheated broiler, as far as possible from the source of heat. Broil on one side for 30 minutes, then turn and baste the top with the juices in the pan. Broil on the other side for another 30 minutes, or until skin is crisp and golden brown. (Lower the heat after 15 minutes if the skin is browning too rapidly.)

The chicken is now ready to serve. It is so good that I never serve a sauce with it, only a large bowl of crisp, green salad and a bottle of chutney. Serves 4.

Chicken Catalan

Another marriage of fresh lemon and chicken — a light, delightful chicken casserole. The Catalans serve it with broiled tomatoes, heavily sprinkled with minced chives, and hot French bread.

> **3 to 4 lb. chicken**
> **4 tbsp. butter**
> **salt and pepper**
> **2 or 3 garlic cloves**
> **3 lemons, unpeeled**
> **¼ tsp. crumbled dried thyme**
> **1 bay leaf**
> **1 cup chicken consommé**
> **1 tbsp. cornstarch**
> **¼ cup cold, heavy cream**

Cut chicken into individual pieces. Heat butter in a casserole and brown the chicken in it. Add salt and pepper to taste.

Crush garlic cloves and add them to the chicken; stir until the garlic starts to brown.

Cut unpeeled lemons into very thin slices. Add to the chicken, together with thyme and bay leaf. Add consommé. Bring to a boil, cover, and cook over medium heat until chicken is tender, 40 to 60 minutes.

Transfer the chicken to a deep, hot serving platter. Arrange the lemon slices over the chicken, but discard the bay leaf. Combine cornstarch and cream. Add to the liquid in the casserole and stir over medium heat until the sauce is creamy and transparent. Strain the sauce over the chicken. Serves 4 to 6.

Monique's Roast Chicken

My daughter, Monique, knows many good tricks for preparing quick, tasty dinners. This is one of her family's favorites.

4 to 6 chicken legs
1 tsp. salt
½ tsp. tarragon or savory
1 tsp. turmeric
¼ tsp. pepper
1 tbsp. flour
½ cup fat (any type)
8 to 12 baking powder biscuits
3 tbsp. flour
⅔ to 1 cup milk

Cut the chicken legs in two. On a plate, or in a paper bag, mix together the salt, tarragon or savory, turmeric, pepper, and flour. Roll the chicken pieces in it. Melt the fat (Monique likes half butter, half bacon fat) in a large baking dish or dripping pan. Place the chicken legs in it and bake for 20 minutes in a 375°F. oven. Turn and bake for another 20 minutes, then move the pieces to one side of the dish.

Meanwhile, prepare the biscuits from a mix or from your own favorite recipe while the chicken is cooking. Place next to the chicken and bake for 15 minutes in a 400°F. oven. Transfer both chicken and biscuits to a hot platter. Add 3 tbsp. of flour to remaining fat in pan. Stir well, add the milk, and cook over direct heat until creamy and smooth. Serve separately, or pour over chicken. Serves 4.

St. Boniface Picnic Broilers

Originally served at French pioneer barn raisings, this delicious method of barbecuing chicken can be easily duplicated using oven broilers.

6 broilers
½ cup salad oil
juice of 2 lemons
½ tsp. salt
½ tsp. marjoram
¼ tsp. pepper
12 to 14 potatoes

The day before the picnic, have the broilers dressed and cut into halves. Brush each half with a mixture of oil, lemon juice, salt, marjoram, and pepper. Lay halves in a waxed-paper-lined roaster or large dish, one on top of the other, and cover with waxed paper. Refrigerate overnight. Before setting out for the picnic, brush again with oil mixture.

At the picnic, when the fire is a gray mass of coals, place chicken, bone side first, on oiled broiler. Brown for 15 minutes, turn, and cook until skin is brown and crisp. Then place pieces in roaster, cover, and put in a just-warm spot on the grill for 15 to 20 minutes. Just before serving, brush the birds with the remaining oil mixture.

Wrap the potatoes in foil and bake in the gray coals for 35 to 40 minutes. Serves 12.

Chicken Livers and Apples

This combination is a new experience in texture and flavor. I often replace the chicken livers with a pound of lamb's liver, cut into finger-sized pieces. Parsleyed rice goes well with this dish.

1 lb. chicken livers
3 tbsp. flour
1 tsp. paprika
½ tsp. each, salt and pepper
⅓ cup butter or margarine
2 tbsp. brandy
1 large onion, finely chopped
4 medium apples, cored and sliced
2 tbsp. brown sugar

Clean chicken livers; halve them. Blend flour, paprika, salt, and pepper. Toss liver in this mixture until well coated.

Sauté liver in 4 tablespoons of the butter over high heat, until brown, stirring all the time. Pour brandy on top. Stir and transfer liver to a hot plate. Put the onion (without any fat) into the same pan and stir, over medium heat, until some of the onion is a golden color. Add to liver.

Add remaining butter to pan, then the apples and sugar; stir, over medium heat, until apples start to soften, about 5 minutes. Combine liver and onions with apples and toss together for a few seconds. Taste for seasoning and serve. Serves 4 to 5.

Chicken Wings "A la Houston"

My friend Houston is a publisher and a great cook. This delicious paella, adapted from the Valencia type, is one of his specialties.

> 5 cups water
> 1 tsp. turmeric
> 1 large onion, chopped
> 3 chicken bouillon cubes
> 1 tbsp. flour
> ½ tsp. salt
> 12 to 24 chicken wings
> ½ cup salad oil
> 1 cup chopped ham or garlic sausage
>   (optional)
> 1 medium onion, minced
> 2 cloves garlic, crushed
> 1 pimiento, diced
> 2 tomatoes, peeled and chopped
> 2 cups uncooked, long grain rice
> 4 cups of prepared bouillon
> 1 can (5 oz.) baby clams
> ½ to 1 small pkg. frozen green peas

Boil together, uncovered, the water, turmeric, large onion, and chicken bouillon cubes until reduced to 4 cups.

Shake in a bag the chicken wings, flour, and salt (use 2 tablespoons flour for 24 wings). Brown in the hot salad oil until crisp. Remove to a large casserole.

Sprinkle the ham or garlic sausage over the chicken wings (optional).

Add the onion, garlic, pimiento, and tomatoes to the fat remaining in the frying pan. Stir together until well blended. Add rice and stir until all is well mixed. Add the 4 cups of reduced bouillon (do not strain), and the juice drained from the clams. Bring to a boil and simmer 5 minutes.

Pour the frozen peas and clams over the chicken wings. Cover and bake for 30 to 40 minutes, in a 350°F. oven until all liquid is absorbed and the rice is tender. Serves 6 to 8.

Quick Tricks with Chicken

Leftover Chicken: Make a "Ritz-looking" salad with leftover greens. To 2 cups diced chicken, add 1 cup diced celery, 1 unpeeled diced apple, a handful of seedless grapes. Blend with ½ to 1 cup mayonnaise. Mix with 3 tablespoons cream, and curry powder to taste. Serve a light, very light, dessert.

Too Many for Your One Barbecued Chicken? Make a casserole. Heat 1 can undiluted consommé. Place in it your cut-up (in many pieces) barbecued chicken, 1 box frozen peas (in frozen state). Cover and simmer until hot. Line casserole with a 2 to 3-inch layer of that already-cooked rice you have in your refrigerator. Pour chicken, green peas, and consommé on top. Add 1 can mushroom soup mixed with ½ cup cream. Bake 25 minutes in 350°F. oven, and you are ready to serve 6 instead of 2.

Your Own Pâté Maison: Fun to serve with Melba toast, when having drinks in the garden. Sauté 5 minutes in butter some chicken livers and minced onion to taste. Then put them through food grinder with 2 hard-boiled eggs. Season with salt, pepper, and tarragon or curry, and why not a tablespoon of brandy or Scotch?

Meats

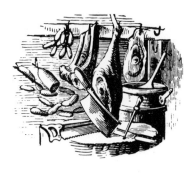

5

Chinese Pepper Steak

This colorful, tasty dish totals only 281 calories per portion, which means you can indulge in a small serving of boiled rice but still have a slimming yet satisfying meal.

> 1 lb. lean top sirloin
> 1 cup celery, thinly sliced on bias
> 1 large onion, thinly sliced
> 1 garlic clove, crushed
> 2 or 3 green peppers, cut into thin slivers
> 1 tbsp. salad oil
> 1 cup bouillon or canned undiluted consommé
> 1 tbsp. cornstarch blended with
> ¼ cup water
> 2 tbsp. soya sauce

Slice the meat very thinly, then cut into thin strips. Make sure all the vegetables are prepared before you start to cook; this dish will be ready to serve in 8 to 10 minutes.

Heat salad oil in large frying pan. Add beef and sear quickly over high heat, stirring most of the time. This will take only 1 minute — remove beef from pan while it is still rare.

Add vegetables and consommé to pan and stir over high heat for 3 to 4 minutes until tender-crisp. Add cornstarch, blended with water and soya sauce, stirring until creamy. When very hot, add beef and reheat for a minute. Serves 4.

French Braised Beef

This thick round steak with its intriguing flavor becomes a company dish when served with *pommes vertes:* equal quantities of mashed pota-

toes and cooked spinach, beaten together until pale green, then seasoned to taste.

> 2½ to 3 lb. piece bottom round of beef
> 2 tbsp. salad oil
> 6 thin slices side bacon or fat salt pork, diced
> paprika, to taste
> 4 carrots, cut into 1-inch pieces
> 4 onions, thinly sliced
> 2 whole cloves, finely chopped
> ½ tsp. thyme
> ¼ tsp. sage
> peel of 1 orange, cut into slivers and white part removed

Remove and dice all visible fat from the beef while heating electric frying pan to 350°F. Heat fat, oil, and bacon or salt pork in pan, and, when suet is brown, sprinkle one side of meat with paprika and place that side in the fat. Brown until golden, then sprinkle other side with paprika, turn and brown, 20 to 25 minutes in all.

Add carrots, onions broken into rings, and seasonings, being careful that there be no white on the orange skin. Season with salt and pepper to taste. Swish it all together a bit, and cook, covered, at 325°F. for 1½ hours, or, until meat is tender.

Remove meat to a hot serving platter. To thicken sauce, either mash the vegetables with the pan juices, or pass them through a sieve and return to pan with half a cup of sour cream. Reheat, but do not let sauce boil; pour over meat. Serves 8.

Boiled Beef Vinaigrette

Periodically, I serve boiled beef, which should actually be called simmered beef, as it must never boil; the meat will then be tender and compact instead of dry and stringy. The contrast of hot meat and cold sauce gives this dish its special character.

  3 to 4 lbs. beef brisket or 4 lbs. short ribs, in
    one piece
  3 celery ribs, cut into 2-inch lengths
  6 carrots, cut into halves
  6 whole onions
  6 small whole parsnips
  ½ tsp. ground thyme
  1 bay leaf
  2 tsp. salt
  ¼ tsp. pepper
  8 to 10 small new potatoes
  ¼ cup cider or tarragon vinegar
  ½ cup minced parsley
  3 tbsp. minced dill
  2 tbsp. minced chives
  2 tsp. salt
  ½ tsp. pepper
  ¼ tsp. dry mustard
  ½ tsp. sugar
  ½ cup olive oil

Put the meat into a large saucepan. Add the celery, carrots, onions, parsnips, thyme, bay leaf, and seasonings. Cover with boiling water. Cover tightly and simmer gently for 4 to 5 hours, or until meat is tender.

About 30 minutes before the meat is ready, transfer 2 to 3 cups of the bouillon to another saucepan. Scrub the potatoes and cook them in their jackets in the extra bouillon.

If it is more convenient the vinaigrette can be prepared a few hours ahead — combine the remaining ingredients and stir for a minute or two.

Set the meat on a hot platter; arrange the carrots, onions, parsnips, and potatoes around the meat. Pour a few spoonfuls of the vinaigrette over the meat and serve the rest cold in an attractive bowl. Serves about 8.

Chuck Steak Braised in Wine

A low-cost cut becomes *haute cuisine* when prepared as follows. Especially good served with baked potatoes and onions that are cooked for the same length of time as the meat in the oven.

The orange and chili sauce give this dish an interesting piquancy.

  3 to 3½ lbs. thick chuck steak
  1 large onion, thinly sliced
  1 small carrot, thinly sliced
  1 cup red wine (any type)
  ½ tsp. each, basil and thyme
  2 tbsp. brown sugar
  3 tbsp. beef or bacon fat
  1 or 2 cloves garlic, chopped fine
    salt and pepper, to taste
  2 tbsp. flour
  1 tbsp. chili sauce
    juice of 1 orange
    chopped parsley or chives

Put the steak in a bowl, top with the onion, carrot, red wine, basil and thyme. Cover and marinate overnight. When ready to cook remove the meat from mixture, wipe it off, and reserve the marinade.

Melt the brown sugar and fat together in a heavy metal frying pan. Sear the meat in it, on all sides, over medium heat. Then transfer meat to a casserole or a Dutch oven. Meanwhile, put the marinade mixture into the frying pan. Heat, scraping the bottom of the pan. When it boils, pour it over the meat. Add the garlic, salt, and pepper to taste. Cover and bake for half an hour in a 325°F. oven. Turn the heat down to 300°F. and bake 1 hour more. Turn the meat over and bake 1½ hours longer or until meat is tender. Remove the meat from the pan. Combine the flour, chili sauce, and orange juice. Add to sauce, whisk thoroughly, then put the sauce through a sieve or, if you prefer, leave the sauce with vegetables in it. Bring to boil while stirring. Pour a few spoonfuls over the meat. Sprinkle top with parsley or chives. Serve the rest of the sauce separately. Serves 8.

Quick Tricks with Beef

Cold Roast Beef: Slice thinly, oh, so thinly. Serve with a basket of lace potatoes and pot of good strong mustard. To make lace potatoes: Grate and mix together 1 raw potato (wash, do not bother to peel), 1 onion (bother to peel), and drop mixture by spoonfuls into sizzling butter or bacon fat, ½ minute each side — then they are cooked and so pretty.

The Hamburger We Have Forgotten: Shape freshly ground round steak (ground only once) into 4-inch rounds, about ¼ inch thick. Wrap each one in freezing paper and freeze. Also keep in freezer split onion or poppy seed buns, the large kind. For a quick lunch in the garden, place frozen buns in 400°F. oven. Unwrap minced steak, season with salt, pepper, paprika, monosodium glutamate. Cook quickly in hot butter, still frozen, 5, 8, or 10 minutes for rare, medium, or well-done. Or, you can barbecue them. Transfer to hot buns, choose your garnish, and enjoy with hot or cold tea.

French Beef Salad

I just love this salad! Make it at least 2 hours before serving, or, even better, 6 to 8 hours before serving.

    3 tbsp. wine or cider vinegar
    1 tsp. salt
    ¼ tsp. pepper
    1 tsp. Dijon Mustard or 1 tsp. dry English
        mustard
    6 tbsp. peanut oil
    2 tbsp. capers, drained (optional)
        a small clove garlic, crushed or ⅛ tsp.
        powdered garlic
    3 tbsp. chopped parsley
    1 onion, red or white, mild, thinly sliced
    8 to 10 slices cold roast beef or pot roast or 3
        cups of same, diced or a mixture of cooked
        meats

Combine in bowl the vinegar, salt, pepper, and mustard. Stir until thoroughly mixed. Beat in the oil, capers, garlic, and 1 tablespoon of the parsley. Beat for 1 minute. Spread the meat in a single layer on a meat platter. Scatter onion rings on top and pour the prepared dressing over all. Cover and marinate at room temperature for at least 2 hours before serving; otherwise keep refrigerated. Sprinkle with the rest of the chopped parsley when ready to serve. Serves 4.

Super Hamburger

To obtain perfect results, follow directions very carefully, as these hamburgers are so good when well made, that they can be served even to the most discriminating guest. In the summer, they are particularly good barbecued, with roasted fresh corn.

    2 lbs. round steak
        3-inch square of beef suet
    1 tsp. seasoned salt
    1 tsp. plain salt
    ½ tsp. freshly ground pepper
    3 tbsp. minced parsley
    ½ tsp. minced fresh or dried thyme
    2 cups red wine

Have the butcher pass both the steak and suet three times through the chopper.

As soon as you get home, put the mixture in a bowl and add the seasoned salt, plain salt, pepper, parsley, and thyme. Mix lightly with a fork. Pour the red wine over, but do not mix. Cover and refrigerate all day.

When ready to cook, mix the wine with the meat. Shape into 6 large, flat patties. Brown in butter; do not overcook. Serve with hot French bread and a green salad. Serves 6.

Cold Beef Salad

The French, Italians, and Mexicans make similar beef salads; this one is originally Greek. It is an excellent way to use up leftover beef.

    1-2 lbs. thinly sliced cold roast or boiled beef
    1 very thinly sliced mild onion
    2 tbsp. capers
    3 tbsp. minced parsley
    ½ tsp. marjoram
    ¼ cup salad oil
    ⅛ cup cider vinegar
    1 tsp. prepared mustard
    ½ tsp. salt

Place the sliced meat in a deep platter. Break the onion into rings and sprinkle on top of meat; then sprinkle with the capers, then with parsley and marjoram.

Mix together the remaining ingredients, shake well, and pour over the salad. Cover loosely and let stand for 3 hours, then refrigerate if you are not ready to serve. Garnish with lettuce or watercress. Serves 6.

Boiled English Kidney Pudding

This pudding may seem difficult to prepare, but, once done, you will realize how easy it is. A perfect cold-weather dish, it is traditionally English.

1½ lbs. bottom round steak
1 beef kidney
1 tbsp. flour
1 onion, finely chopped
1¾ cups flour
½ tsp. salt
¼ cup fresh white bread crumbs
1 cup minced beef suet

Cut the beef and kidneys into half-inch cubes. Roll them in 1 tbsp. of flour mixed with salt and pepper to taste, mix in onion, and set aside.

To make suet-crust pastry, sift flour with salt into bowl. Add bread crumbs and stir in suet. Mix to a firm dough with about ½ cup of cold water. Grease a 1½-pint English pudding dish (a round, white bowl with a wide rim).

On a floured board, roll two-thirds of the pastry into a circle about 1-inch thick. Dust center with flour, then fold circle in half. Make a 1-inch pleat in the middle of curved side, turn over, and do the same on the other side — so that the dough will fit the round dish. Press bottom fold, rolling pin from bottom of pastry to top, not from side to side.

Lift one edge of the pastry and put your fist inside the pocket — when removed it will be the familiar "bonnet" you have seen professional cooks achieve. Lay pudding bowl on its side and carefully place pastry in it. Straighten bowl, and, starting at the pleats, work edge of pastry so that it stands ½ to 1 inch above the top of the dish. Pour in meat mixture and add cold water until dish is three-quarters full. Dampen edge of pastry, roll a lid out of remaining piece, place on pudding, and pinch edges together well.

Dip a piece of clean cotton cloth into hot water and wring it out. Flour the inside, make a 1-inch pleat in the middle to allow for rising, and cover pudding with it. Tie string around rim, then loosely knot four corners of cloth back over top.

Submerge pudding in a large pan of rapidly boiling water, cover pan, and boil steadily for 3 to 4 hours. If necessary, add more hot water; the pudding should be covered by an inch or two of water at all times.

To serve, take off cloth and tie a folded napkin around dish. Set it on the table with a jug of boiling water, and, after the first portion of pudding has been cut, pour in a little water to increase and dilute the very rich, tasty gravy.

Scottish Beef and Kidney Pie

This is quite different from the English beef and kidney pie. Often the beef kidney is replaced by 3 or 4 lamb kidneys, or 2 veal kidneys. If you have a little porcelain blackbird to use as a funnel, you will be really traditional.

pie crust of your choice
1½ lbs. bottom round steak
1 small beef kidney
flour
1 tbsp. butter
1 large onion, chopped
1¼ cups boiling water
1 tsp. salt
¼ tsp. pepper
1 tbsp. Worcestershire sauce
1 tbsp. strong prepared mustard
2 tbsp. flour

Remove and reserve all fat from the steak and cut meat into three-quarter-inch cubes. Cut kidney into one-quarter-inch cubes and roll both the steak and kidney pieces in flour.

Melt fat (from the steak) in a large frying pan, add butter, and fry onion until golden brown. With heat on high, gradually add beef and kidney pieces, until all rawness disappears, then transfer to a heavy metal saucepan.

Add remaining ingredients to the fat left in pan; bring to a boil while stirring; pour over meat. Cover and simmer for 1 hour, or until meat is tender. Cool and, if you wish to de-fat the sauce, refrigerate overnight. The next day, remove the fat and proceed.

Place a small funnel or a pie bird in the center of a deep, 10-inch round baking dish, preferably one with a half-inch rim. Pour the meat and about half the gravy down the funnel. Roll enough pastry to cover the top, making a hole in the middle to pass over the funnel or bird, and brush with milk. Bake in a 425°F. oven for 30 to 35 minutes, or until golden brown. Reheat leftover gravy and serve in sauceboat. Serves 6.

Finnish Jellied Tongue

A Finnish friend taught me how to cook this superb dish made with jellied sour cream and garnished with feathery stems of fresh dill. It is a refreshing change from the usual meat dish served at buffet dinners.

1 fresh beef tongue
2 tbsp. sugar
1 tbsp. coarse salt
6 to 8 cups hot water
1 bay leaf
1 unpeeled lemon, thinly sliced
5 or 6 slices fresh ginger root or 1 tsp. ground ginger
1 quart cold water
3 tbsp. coarse salt
1 tbsp. sugar
1 envelope unflavored gelatin
  juice of 1 lemon
1 cup sour cream
  fresh dill or parsley

Mix together the 2 tbsp. sugar and the 1 tbsp. salt and rub evenly over the tongue. Cover, and refrigerate overnight.

The next day, put the tongue in a large saucepan, add the hot water, bay leaf, sliced lemon, ginger root or ground ginger. Bring to a fast rolling boil, skim off the foam, cover and simmer over low heat for 2 to 3 hours until the tongue is tender. Skin the tongue while hot and let it cool in its broth.

In the meantime, bring 1 quart cold water to a boil with 3 tbsp. salt and 1 tbsp. sugar. Cool, then pour over the cooled tongue. Refrigerate for 12 hours. Drain thoroughly and transfer to a flat platter.

Soak the unflavored gelatin in the lemon juice for 5 minutes and then dissolve it over hot water. Slowly add it to the sour cream, while stirring, and spread the cold tongue with this cream. Garnish with sprigs of fresh dill or parsley and refrigerate for 1 hour to set the gelatin. To serve, slice thinly. Serves 6 to 8.

Smoked Beef Tongue

This is an excellent dish for a buffet supper, because it can be kept warm in a chafing dish. The tongue can be cooked days ahead of time, then sliced and simmered in the wine-cranberry sauce. Serve it with rice, noodles, or pan-fried potatoes.

1 smoked beef tongue (about 2 lbs.)
1-inch piece of fresh ginger root (optional)
3 slices unpeeled lemon
2 bay leaves
½ tsp. peppercorns
½ cup dark brown sugar
1 cup fresh cooked cranberries or canned sauce plus juice or half a lemon
12 whole cloves
¼ cup dry red wine or sherry
½ unpeeled lemon, thinly sliced

Wash tongue, cover with cold water, and let stand 3 to 5 hours. Drain, place in a saucepan with enough cold water to cover, the ginger root (do not use powdered), 3 lemon slices, bay leaves, and peppercorns. Bring to a boil, cover, and simmer over low heat for 3 to 4 hours or until tender (it is cooked when the skin can be removed). Cool, then cut off back part of tongue. If cooking ahead of time, wrap and refrigerate until ready to use.

Simmer brown sugar, cranberries, cloves, and wine or sherry for 5 minutes. Add lemon slices and paper-thin slices of cooked tongue. Keep warm over low heat. Serves 6 to 8.

Lamb Rack Orientale

However odd this recipe may sound, follow directions to the letter — the result will amaze you. It will be in keeping with the high standard one expects from this excellent cut of lamb.

1½ to 2½ lb. rack of lamb
⅓ cup teriyaki sauce (Universal Kikoman is excellent)
2 tbsp. orange marmalade
1 tbsp. grated, fresh ginger root
1 clove garlic, crushed

Place rack in a standing position in a small roasting pan. Preheat oven to 325°F. Set pan in oven. Roast 40 minutes without disturbing it. (Whatever the weight of the rack of lamb, the roasting time is 40 minutes.)

Meanwhile, combine the remaining ingredients. When the 40 minutes is up, pour this mixture over the lamb, turning it a few times to ensure complete coverage. Lower heat to 300°F.; cook lamb for another 20 minutes. Turn off heat and turn the meat, side down, in the sauce. Let stand until ready to serve. Adjust seasonings. Superb!

Always carve a rack of lamb by starting with the partial cuts in the backbones or the heavy bones. Serves 4.

Easter Leg of Lamb

Every Easter Sunday for many years we had dinner at the home of my maternal *grandmère*. She had a very special way with a leg of lamb. Try it, if you like fat-free gravy and tender, moist lamb.

>5 to 6-lb. leg of lamb
>1 cup water
>1 tbsp. butter
>1 onion, stuck with 3 cloves
>1 large carrot, sliced
>2 slices of unpeeled lemon
>2 celery stalks, diced
>8 or 10 parsley sprigs, chopped
>1 tsp. minced basil or oregano
>1 tsp. salt
>½ tsp. pepper
>1 cup consommé (any type)
>½ cup red wine
>½ cup light or heavy cream
>2 tbsp. browned flour

Place the leg of lamb in a roasting pan with the water. Cover and cook over high heat on top of the stove until the water has evaporated.

Uncover, add the butter, and, still over high heat, brown the meat all over. Remove the lamb from the pan and discard all the accumulated fat from it.

Place in the bottom of the pan the onion, carrot, lemon slices, celery, parsley, and basil or oregano. Stir until well mixed. Place the lamb on top of these vegetables. Add salt and pepper to taste. Add the consommé. Cover and simmer over very low heat for 1½ hours.

Blend together the wine, cream, and browned flour. Pour over lamb. Stir around until well mixed with all the ingredients. Cover and simmer for another 30 minutes.

Remove the meat to a hot platter. Strain the gravy and serve it separately. Serves 6 to 8.

Lamb Rack "à la Française"

Quite different from Lamb Rack Orientale, I really cannot say which recipe I like best. Both are excellent.

>1½ to 2½-lb. rack of lamb
>3 tbsp. brandy
>1 tsp. fine Dijon mustard
>½ tsp. fresh or dried tarragon
>¼ tsp. coarsely ground peppercorns
>½ tsp. salt
>2 tbsp. butter
>3 tbsp. dry Madeira
>3 tbsp. chicken broth or water

Place rack of lamb in roasting pan. Set in a preheated 400°F. oven for 20 minutes. Take out of oven, pour brandy on top, and turn the meat around to coat it all with brandy.

Cream together (have it ready when meat is out of oven), the mustard, tarragon, salt, pepper, butter. Spread on top of the rack. Put back in oven.

Roast to 150°F. on meat thermometer (The perfect internal temperature for rack of lamb). Remove meat to a hot platter. Place roasting pan on direct heat; add the Madeira, chicken broth or water to the drippings. Bring to a boil while scraping the bottom of the pan. Strain the sauce into hot sauceboat and serve separately. Serves 4.

Mint-Peppercorn Roast Shoulder of Lamb

When I make this dish, I make the required cup of broth from bones removed from the shoulder. Use Malabar black peppercorns, if possible. They are the most perfumed and flavorful.

>1 whole shoulder of lamb
>8 to 10 peppercorns
>1 tsp. salt
>¼ cup salad oil or melted butter
>1 bunch green onions, coarsely chopped
>8 stalks fresh mint, coarsely chopped or 1 tbsp. dried mint
>1 cup broth, any type

Thailand Pork Tenderloin — a taste treat from the Orient, colorful and economical. Recipe on page 39.

Preheat the oven to 350°F.

Place the peppercorns in a piece of cotton and crush them with a rolling pin or a potato masher. Place the meat in a dripping pan and rub it all over with the salt and ½ tsp. of the crushed peppercorns.

Roast the meat, uncovered, for 20 minutes, then pour the oil or melted butter on top. Continue roasting uncovered for 20 minutes per pound. Twenty minutes before it is ready, cover the meat with the green onions and mint, then add the broth to the pan.

When the meat is done, remove it from the oven and baste for 1 to 2 minutes with the pan drippings. Place the roast on a hot platter and serve the gravy as is, or, thicken it to taste with 1 tbsp. of flour. Serves 8.

Nanny's Honest Irish Stew

Clara, who was our nanny when we were children, was actually French, but she had an Irish mother. As it turned out, she cared very little for cooking, no doubt because she had her hands full with her boisterous charges. But every now and then a spark of interest would flare up whenever she made one of her mother's "famous" Irish dishes. Clara's mother had brought from Ireland, as part of her dowry, a very special little book containing recipes, meticulously handwritten by her grandmother. Eventually the book was given to Clara, when, as Clara put it, her mother had "left this world to live in glory with the angels." Here is a recipe from Clara's book.

   3 lbs. neck of lamb
  12 medium-sized potatoes
   4 large onions, sliced thick
     salt and pepper
  ½ tsp. ground thyme
   2 cups cold water

Only the neck will do, and so much the better, since it is cheap. It usually comes with lamb-in-the-basket or ask your butcher to reserve 3 pounds of lamb neck in advance — it really is worth the trouble.

Remove excess fat from the meat and then cut into sections through the bones. Your butcher can also do this for you, but do not let him remove the bones as these enhance the flavor.

Peel the potatoes and cut four of them into thin slices, as for scalloped potatoes. Leave the rest whole.

Arrange the sliced potatoes in the bottom of a heavy metal saucepan or casserole, then half of the sliced onions, then the pieces of lamb. Season generously with salt and pepper. Sprinkle the rest of the onions with thyme and arrange them on top of the lamb. Surround them with the whole potatoes. Pour the cold water on top. Cover tightly. Cook in a 350°F. oven for 2½ hours, or simmer over very low heat for the same length of time. The sliced potatoes thicken the juice while the whole potatoes retain their shape and are cooked just right. Makes 6 servings.

Clara used to serve her Irish stew in three small bowls, each filled with capers, good homemade mustard, and chopped parsley or chives.

Note: If it is absolutely impossible to obtain the neck of the lamb, you can replace it with an equal amount of lamb-in-the-basket.

Jack's Barbecued Lamb Shanks

My friend Jack loved beer. He called it the "new flavor dimension."

   2 cloves garlic
   4 to 6 lamb shanks
   3 tbsp. melted lamb fat or bacon fat
   3 tbsp. flour
  ½ tsp. salt
  ½ tsp. freshly ground pepper
  ½ tsp. savory
  ½ cup beer
   2 bay leaves
  ¼ cup fresh lemon juice
     grated peel of half a lemon

Put slivers of the garlic into the lamb shanks, making incisions with a pointed knife. Melt the pieces of lamb fat or heat the bacon fat in a Dutch oven. Blend the flour, salt, pepper, and savory. Roll shanks in flour mixture and brown all over in the hot fat. Then add all the other ingredients. Cover and simmer for 2 hours or until meat is tender. (The more it simmers, the more gravy forms.) Serve it as Jack did, with boiled rice loaded with butter, parsley, and sliced fried mushrooms. Serves 4 to 6.

Hare en Pot, a traditional Quebec recipe, is an aromatic combination of herbs, red wine, currant jelly, and garlic croutons. Recipe on page 42.

Oxtail Casserole

Unusual and very tasty, this casserole can be made two or three days before serving if kept refrigerated. Also, it freezes well for 2 months. Reheat in a preheated 400°F. oven.

2 oxtails, cut into 2-inch pieces
3 tbsp. butter
2 cans undiluted consommé
1 large onion, thinly sliced
1 clove garlic, minced
1 green pepper, diced
1 small can tomatoes
3 small carrots, thinly sliced
1 tsp. salt
6 peppercorns
1 tsp. brown sugar
½ tsp. basil
⅛ tsp. marjoram
    a pinch thyme
1 cup red wine
1 tsp. lemon juice

Brown the oxtails in butter over high heat. Place in an earthenware casserole and cover with the consommé. Brown the onion and the garlic in the butter remaining in the pan. Spread over the oxtails. Add the rest of the ingredients. Cover the casserole and cook in a 325°F. oven for 3 to 4 hours or until the oxtails are tender.

To serve, arrange 6 to 8 small boiled potatoes, rolled in finely minced parsley, around the meat. Serves 4 to 6.

Mushroom Veal Loaf

This loaf can be served either hot or cold. Make it a month ahead and freeze, or a week ahead and refrigerate.

1 lb. veal, minced
1 lb. uncooked ham, minced
4 tbsp. catsup
3 tbsp. chopped green pepper
1 medium-size onion, grated
2 eggs
1 tsp. salt
¼ cup fine, dry bread crumbs
1 cup undiluted mushroom soup
1 cup fresh or canned mushrooms, fried

Thoroughly mix all ingredients except mushrooms; pour half of mixture into a 9 x 5 inch loaf pan. Cover with mushrooms and top with remaining mixture. Bake for 1 hour in a 350°F. oven and cool. Cover with foil and freeze, or refrigerate.

To serve, place in 350°F. oven and bake covered until heated through — about 1 hour if frozen, 40 minutes if refrigerated; unmold. Serves 6.

Veal Chops Toscanini

This dish was created for the great maestro at a dinner that followed the unforgettable Wagner concert he directed in honor of Cosima Wagner, then a very old lady. As a student in Paris at the time, I had the joy of being at the concert and was invited to the superb midnight dinner that followed.

4 thick loin veal chops
4 thin slices of bacon
¾ cup grated Swiss cheese
    pepper
3 tbsp. butter
    salt, to taste
4 ripe tomatoes, peeled
½ tsp. sugar
½ tsp. crumbled dried thyme
    butter
    juice of 1 lemon

In the side of each chop, make an incision large enough to form a sort of small pocket. Dice the bacon; and, for each chop, mix one fourth of the diced bacon with 1 teaspoon of grated cheese. Pepper the inside of the pocket and fill with the bacon and cheese.

Melt the butter in a heavy enamelled cast-iron frying pan. When light brown, add the chops and brown for 5 minutes on each side, turning only once. Add salt and pepper to taste, cover, and cook the chops over very low heat for 15 minutes.

In the meantime, place the peeled whole tomatoes in a shallow baking dish and sprinkle with the sugar and thyme. Place in a 450°F. oven for 5 minutes.

Top each tomato with a veal chop. Pour over the chops any juices accumulated in the pan. Sprinkle the whole with the remaining grated cheese and 8 to 10 small dice of butter. Put back in the oven until the cheese has melted and the chops are a crusty brown on top.

Remove from the oven and pour the lemon juice over the chops. Serves 4.

American Chop Suey

Yes, a pound of boneless pork will serve 4 to 6 people. Take the meat from chops, or use tenderloin.

    1 lb. lean boneless pork
    2 tbsp. salad oil
    ¼ cup hot water
    6 to 8 green onions, cut into 1-inch pieces
    1½ cups celery, thinly sliced
    5-oz. can water chestnuts, thinly sliced
    1 cup chicken broth
    1 tbsp. soya sauce
    1 tbsp. cornstarch

Cut the meat into thin strips. Heat the oil in a large, heavy frying pan; add meat, and stir over medium heat until rawness disappears. Add hot water, cover, and simmer for 20 minutes over low heat.

Add onions, celery, chestnuts, broth, and simmer, covered, for 15 minutes. Add combined soya sauce and cornstarch, stirring until slightly thickened. Taste for seasoning and serve with rice. Serves 4.

Stuffed Roast Pork Tenderloin

Pork tenderloin is an ideal cut when a small roast is required. It is equally good hot or cold.

    1¼ to 1½ lbs. pork tenderloin
    ½ recipe for Citrus Dressing (page 63)
    ½ tsp. salt
    ¼ tsp. pepper
    ½ tsp. curry powder

Beat the tenderloin with the flat side of a cleaver to flatten it, then slit in half, without separating the two pieces. Fill with dressing and tie securely.

Mix the salt, pepper, and curry powder. Rub seasonings all over the meat. Place on a well-oiled roasting pan (without a rack) and insert a meat thermometer into its center. Do not cover the

meat; do not wrap in foil; do not add water. Bake in a 325°F. oven until the thermometer registers 185°F., or, for 35 minutes per pound.

Serve with browned potatoes and broccoli with butter and lemon juice. Serves 4.

Chinese Braised Loin of Pork

Use a cast iron or an electric frying pan to cook this dish. The meat glazes to a deep brown color and has an intriguing flavor, without being too exotic.

    3 to 4 lb. loin of pork
    1 finely chopped garlic clove
    1 tsp. salt
    ¼ tsp. pepper
    2 tbsp. honey
    ¼ cup soya sauce
    1 cup beef broth
    2 tbsp. dry sherry

Bone the loin by detaching the meat from the bones and tying it into a neat roll, or you can leave the bone in if you prefer.

Rub the pork with a mixture of the garlic, salt, and pepper. Brown it over medium heat on all sides, beginning with the fat side. Mix remaining ingredients, bring to a boil, and pour over meat. Cover and cook over low (250°F. to 300°F.) heat for 1½ hours, or until tender, basting 3 or 4 times during cooking. Serve with plain or fried rice. Serves 6.

Thailand Pork Tenderloin

This is a colorful and tasty dish. One tenderloin can serve 6, simply by adding more vegetables to the recipe.

    1 or 2 pork tenderloins
    2 eggs, beaten
    3 tbsp. cornstarch
    1 carrot, cut into thin shreds
    1 green pepper, cut into thin shreds
    ½ cup slivered celery
    2 tbsp. sugar
    2 tbsp. vinegar
    1 bouillon cube
    1 cup hot water
    4 tbsp. salad oil

Cut the tenderloin into half-inch cubes. Roll them in the beaten eggs and then the cornstarch. Set on wax paper to dry.

Place the vegetables, sugar, vinegar, bouillon cube, and hot water in a bowl, stirring to dissolve the bouillon cube. Set aside for 30 minutes. (Use more vegetables if you have only one tenderloin).

Heat the oil in a large frying pan. Add the pieces of tenderloin and brown quickly over high heat, stirring all the time. Add the vegetable mixture and stir for 2 or 3 minutes over medium heat. Serve immediately, with a bowl of boiled rice. Serves 4.

Coated Roast Pork

The coating, low heat, and long cooking period seal in the juices and result in a tender, tasty roast.

> 2 to 3 lbs. shoulder of pork
> 4 tbsp. soya sauce
> 1 tbsp. sherry
> 1 tbsp. cornstarch
> 1/4 tsp. pepper
> 1/4 tsp. monosodium glutamate
> 2 garlic cloves, crushed

Preheat the oven to 275°F. and place roast on a rack in a dripping pan.

Blend together the remaining ingredients and spread this mixture over the entire surface of the meat. Roast 45 to 50 minutes per pound. The meat will then be crisp on the outside, but tender and juicy on the inside. Serve either hot or cold. Serves 4 to 6.

Barbecued Spareribs

A most versatile recipe — cook the rib in one piece or cut it into 2-inch pieces; bake or broil in the oven, or barbecue over charcoal. The flavor and crispness, although different in each case, are just right.

> 1 or 2 cloves garlic, crushed
> 1/2 cup soya sauce
> 1/3 cup sugar or honey
> 1 tbsp. grated orange peel
> 1 tsp. salt
> 1/4 tsp. pepper
> 2 1/2 to 3 lbs. spareribs

Mix garlic, soya sauce, sugar or honey, orange peel, salt, and pepper.

Trim excess fat from spareribs; use pieces whole or cut into 2-inch lengths. Place meat in a shallow pan, spread with the garlic mixture. Let stand covered in refrigerator, 1 to 24 hours, turning meat 2 or 3 times.

To broil the meat: Place whole piece, curved side down, on rack in baking pan. If the meat is cut, position the squares next to each other. Preheat broiler to 325°F. for 15 minutes; then broil (with the pan 6 to 8 inches from the element) for about 20 minutes. When meat is crusty and brown on one side, turn it and continue cooking until the other side has browned and is tender.

To bake: Place rib or ribs in shallow dripping pan, without rack, in 400°F. oven.

Broiled or baked, cooking time is 40 to 60 minutes. Serves 4.

Stuffed Spareribs

I have never been able to decide whether I like this recipe better hot or cold. Either way these ribs are superb. If you wish, roast them early in the morning, arrange them on a platter, cover with foil and let stand until dinner time. They will be tepid, moist, and oh, so good!

> 3 to 4 lbs. pork spareribs
> 1 tsp. salt
> 1/4 tsp. pepper
> 2 1/2 cups bread, diced
> 3 tbsp. soft butter
> 2 eggs
>   salt and pepper, to taste
> 1 tsp. sage or savory
> 1/4 cup parsley, chopped
> 2 cups cider or water

Use a whole rack of spareribs or two of equal size. Rub them with salt and pepper. In a bowl, combine the bread, butter, eggs, salt, pepper, sage or savory, and parsley. Mix well and put on top of the spareribs. If cooking one rack of ribs, fold it over and sew the ends together, or, secure the ends with skewers. With two pieces, put stuffing on one piece and cover with the other. Tie together with string.

Transfer the whole to a roasting pan containing the cider or water. Bake at 450°F. for 1 hour, turning every 20 minutes. If meat browns too much, turn heat down to 350°F. Serves 6.

Rum Ham

The combination of rum, oranges, and brown sugar makes a delicious glaze. Even though the ham takes time to cook, it requires only a little attention, which makes it a good dish for a party, especially a buffet.

> 1 ham, any size
> 1 or 2 tsp. whole cloves
> 1 cup brown sugar
> 3 oranges, unpeeled
> 1½ cups rum

Wrap a ham in heavy-duty foil. Bake in a 300°F. oven for 35 minutes to the pound. (Any size ham can be baked this way.)

About 1 hour before ham is done, remove from the foil. Remove the rind with a sharp knife and score the fat. Stud with cloves. Pack brown sugar on top.

Slice unpeeled oranges. Place them in the bottom of the baking pan. Set the ham on the bed of oranges. Slowly, pour the rum over the ham.

Return the pan to the oven for 1 hour. Baste ham a few times with the liquid in the pan. A 6-lb., boneless, fully cooked ham will serve 8 to 10.

Ham Loaf

Serve this loaf thinly sliced, with fresh Onion Cucumber Relish and rye bread, and assorted fruits and cheeses for dessert. A great meal!

> 1½ lbs. ground, cooked or uncooked ham
> ¾ lb. ground fresh pork
> 3 eggs, slightly beaten
> ½ cup undiluted cream of celery soup
> ½ tsp. marjoram or curry powder
> ½ tsp. dry mustard
> 1 cup dry bread crumbs

Mix all the ingredients, in the order given. (No salt is needed as the ham and soup are salty enough.) Put into a 9 x 5 inch loaf pan and bake uncovered in a 350°F. oven for 1¼ hours. Cool, cover, and refrigerate (it will keep for 4 days) or freeze (3 months).

To reheat, thaw completely and heat, uncovered in a 350°F. oven for 30 minutes. Serves 6.

Greek Pikti

Pikti are the jellied pigs' feet of Greece, very similar to the pork head cheese of Quebec, although more delicate in flavor. They are served either as appetizers or as a main course.

> 4 pigs' feet, cut up
> 1 tbsp. salt
> 4 onions, sliced
> 2 carrots, whole
> 1 cup celery, chopped
> 1 bay leaf
> 3 whole cloves
> 1 tsp. peppercorns
> ½ tsp. oregano
> ½ cup pimiento, diced
> 3 tbsp. cider or wine vinegar
> ½ cup fresh parsley, minced

Place the pigs' feet in a large saucepan and cover with boiling water. Add the salt. Cover and simmer for 2 hours, then remove any scum that has accumulated on top.

Add the onions, carrots, celery, bay leaf, cloves, peppercorns, and oregano. Bring back to a boil, cover, and simmer for 1 hour, or until the meat is falling from the bones. Remove the meat and the carrots from the bouillon and set aside.

Strain the broth, pour it back into the pan, and boil until reduced by one third. Pick the meat from the bones and chop coarsely or finely, according to taste. Do not discard the skin; chop it with the rest of the meat. Dice the carrots and add, with the pimiento, to the meat. Pour it all into the reduced broth and simmer together for 5 minutes.

Remove from heat, add the vinegar and parsley, and pour into 3 or 4 molds. Cool, cover, and refrigerate until firm. To serve, unmold and garnish with parsley and lemon quarters. Serves 8 to 10.

Hare en Pot

Québecois and Vermonters share many a traditional recipe — this is one. Similar to English jugged hare, it is a superb hot casserole for a buffet dinner.

3 to 4 lb. hare or rabbit
6 tbsp. flour
1 tsp. salt
¼ tsp. pepper
1 tsp. brown sugar
1 tsp. savory
4 tbsp. butter
5 or 6 slices bacon
1 onion, stuck with 3 cloves
rind 1 lemon, grated
6 peppercorns
1 bay leaf
2 tbsp. minced parsley stems
1½ cups water or light red wine
2 tbsp. red currant jelly
garlic croutons

Cut the hare or rabbit into 6 or 8 pieces. Roll in 4 tablespoons of the flour mixed with salt, pepper, brown sugar, and savory.

Brown the floured pieces in butter. Line a casserole dish with bacon slices, and put the pieces of browned hare on top.

Add the onion, stuck with cloves, grated lemon rind, peppercorns, bay leaf, and minced parsley stems. Pour 1¼ cups of the water, or light red wine, on top. Do not mix.

Cover and cook in a 325°F. oven for 2 hours, or until the hare is tender.

Transfer hare pieces to a hot dish. Thicken the gravy with the remaining 2 tablespoons flour mixed with the remaining ¼ cup red wine or water. When the gravy is creamy, add currant jelly. Taste and add more seasoning if necessary. Pour gravy over the hare and garnish with garlic croutons. Serves 6 to 8.

Grains and Pasta

6

Maple Syrup Baked Beans

This is one of my family's recipes. I have never seen the apple topping in any cookbook, and have no idea where my mother got the idea — maybe it was her own. These are very, very, good beans.

4 cups dried navy beans
12 cups cold water
1 tsp. soda
1 lb. fat and lean salt pork, sliced
1 large onion
1 tsp. dry mustard
1 cup maple syrup
1 tbsp. coarse salt
4 cored apples, unpeeled
1 cup maple or light brown sugar
½ cup butter
½ cup rum (optional)

Preheat oven to 325°F.

Cover the beans with 12 cups cold water. Soak overnight. In the morning, pour the whole thing in a large saucepan. Add 1 teaspoon soda and more cold water to cover the beans, if necessary. Bring to a boil, uncovered, then boil until some of the skins come off when you blow on the beans.

Line a bean pot with the sliced pork, then pour in the beans and their water. Roll the onion in the dry mustard until all of the mustard sticks to it; bury it in the middle of the beans. Pour the maple syrup and coarse salt on top.

Bake 4 to 5 hours in a 325°F. oven. In the last hour of cooking, cover the beans with the whole apples, placed as closely together as possible. Cream the sugar and butter together, then spread the mixture on top of the apples. This forms a most delicious topping when the beans are baked. Pour the rum on top just before serving. Serves 8 to 10.

Buckwheat Kasha Casserole

If you like the flavor of buckwheat, you will love this casserole — excellent for lunch with a green salad.

1 box medium buckwheat kasha
2 to 3 tbsp. butter
    salt, pepper, to taste
1 to 2 cups cottage cheese
2 eggs
3 to 4 green onions, chopped (optional)

Cook the box of buckwheat kasha according to directions on the box. When done, add the butter, salt, and pepper.

Place half of it in a deep casserole. Mix together the cottage cheese, eggs, and green onions. Spread over kasha. Top with the rest of the kasha.

Bake, uncovered, in a 350°F. oven for 20 to 25 minutes. Serves 6.

Green Noodles Toscana

Any type of pasta can replace the green noodles. One has to make this tomato sauce to fully appreciate the perfection of taste and color.

2 to 3 large ripe tomatoes
1 tsp. sugar
1 tbsp. butter or olive oil
8 ounces green noodles
1 cup grated Parmesan or cheddar cheese

Chop unpeeled tomatoes into chunks (if you prefer, peel tomatoes before cooking). Place in saucepan, cook, uncovered, over a brisk fire, until thick and creamy (about 15 minutes for 3 tomatoes). Add sugar. Stir well. Remove from heat and stir in the butter or oil, which will turn the sauce into a creamy purée.

Cook noodles according to package directions. Serve with the grated cheese. Serves 4.

Meatless Lasagne

This is my daughter's large recipe, to serve 10. Make it in one dish, or, prepare two casseroles, serve one, and freeze the other.

20 cups water
1 tbsp. each, salt and salad oil
1 lb. (16 oz.) lasagne noodles
2 lbs. cottage cheese
1 cup commercial sour cream
2 eggs
½ tsp. pepper
½ tsp. oregano
1 lb. Mozzarella cheese, thinly sliced
3 tbsp. salad oil
2 large onions, chopped fine
¼ cup celery, chopped fine
1 (28-oz.) can tomatoes
2 (6-oz.) cans tomato paste
¼ tsp. pepper
1 tsp. basil
2 tsp. sugar
2 (4-oz.) cans chopped mushrooms or 1½ lbs. ground beef

Bring water to boil in soup kettle. Add the salt and salad oil. Then add the lasagne noodles, one by one, and boil for 10 to 15 minutes or until tender. When ready, pour cold water into the pot until noodles are cold enough to be handled, but do not drain.

While the lasagne cooks and cools, prepare the following mixtures:

Mix the cottage cheese, sour cream, eggs, pepper, oregano, and salt to taste. Butter a large oblong dish or 28-inch casserole.

Slice the Mozzarella and set aside.

Now make the mushroom sauce. Heat 2 tablespoons of the oil in large frying pan, add the onions and celery; stir until lightly browned. Strain tomatoes to remove seeds, pressing down the pulp. Add to onions. Add tomato paste, pepper, basil, and sugar. Boil for 10 minutes.

Heat remaining tablespoon of oil. Add the drained mushrooms. Stir until hot. Add to sauce. Taste for seasoning. Then assemble casserole in a large baking dish or divide between two casseroles. Place a layer of noodles in long strips to cover the bottom. Next, a layer of the cottage cheese mixture, then slices of Mozzarella, then mushroom sauce. Repeat these layers until dish is filled, ending with noodles, sauce, and topping of sliced cheese.

Bake either size dish in a preheated 325°F. oven for 1½ hours. Refrigerate or freeze, covered, without baking. To serve, bake at 350°F. for 1½ hours. Serves 10.

Cheddar Baked Macaroni

The personality of this baked macaroni is in the combination of grated and diced cheddar. Use strong, old cheddar. The tossed bread crumbs on top can be covered with an additional half cup of diced cheddar or Swiss cheese.

16 oz. elbow macaroni
1 cup grated cheddar cheese
1 cup diced cheddar cheese
3 tbsp. butter
½ cup celery, cut into small dice
1 onion, minced
4 tbsp. flour
2 cups milk
1 cup light cream
salt and pepper, to taste
½ cup dry bread crumbs
1 tbsp. melted butter

Cook macaroni according to directions on package; drain and place half the macaroni in a buttered baking dish. Sprinkle with half of the grated and half the diced cheese. Add the rest of the macaroni and cover with the rest of the cheese.

Melt the butter, add the celery and onion; simmer for 10 minutes over low heat. Add the flour; mix, then add the milk and cream, cook until creamy. Salt and pepper to taste. Pour over the macaroni. Toss the bread crumbs with the melted butter and sprinkle over the macaroni. Bake for 40 minutes, uncovered, in a 350°F. oven. Serves 6.

My Noodle Casserole

When I can't think of what to cook for a light meal, I often prepare this simple but tasty casserole.

    8 oz. noodles
 1¼ cups plain yogurt or sour cream
    8 oz. cottage cheese
 ¼ cup butter or margarine
 ½ tsp. salt
 ¼ tsp. pepper
    4 tbsp. chopped parsley
    3 green onions, chopped (optional)
    1 egg, lightly beaten

Cook noodles according to package directions, then drain. Put back into pan with remaining ingredients and stir with a fork over low heat until thoroughly heated. Pour into a 1½-quart casserole (you can prepare this ahead of time) and bake, uncovered, in 300°F. oven for 45 minutes. Serves 6.

The Easiest of All Tomato Macaroni

I have had so many requests for this recipe that it is a pleasure to pass it on to you. It is equally good hot or cold. Cold, I like to serve it with thinly sliced cold roast beef or a green salad.

 20-oz. can tomatoes
    1 tbsp. sugar
    1 tsp. dry mustard
 ½ tsp. pepper
 ¼ tsp. thyme or ½ tsp. savory
 ¼ to ½ cup celery leaves, finely chopped
    1 tsp. paprika
    6-oz. can tomato paste
 ½ lb. macaroni, cooked
 ½ lb. cheese, grated
    bread crumbs
    butter

Pour ⅓ of the canned tomatoes into a well-buttered casserole or baking dish. To the remaining tomatoes, add the sugar, dry mustard, pepper, thyme or savory, celery leaves, paprika, and tomato paste. Mix together thoroughly.

Make alternate layers of the tomato mixture, macaroni, and grated cheese; sprinkle with bread crumbs and dot with butter. Bake in a 350°F. oven for 35 to 45 minutes. Serves 6.

Eggplant Sauce

The time to make this sauce is from June to September, when eggplant and green pepper are readily available.

    1 medium-size eggplant, peeled and diced
    2 tbsp. bacon fat
    1 garlic clove, chopped
    1 green pepper, chopped
 ½ tsp. basil
 24-oz. can tomatoes
    1 tsp. salt
 ¼ tsp. pepper
 ½ lb. spaghetti or elbow macaroni, cooked

Soak the eggplant in cold water for 10 minutes and drain well. Heat fat, add garlic, green pepper, basil, and cook over low heat until vegetables are tender. Add tomatoes, salt, pepper, and eggplant, and simmer uncovered over medium heat for one hour.

Mix with hot pasta and serve with a bowl of grated cheese of your choice. Serves 4 to 5.

Red Wine Spaghetti Sauce

Chianti is, of course, the best choice for a spaghetti sauce, but any red wine will do. This sauce is a specialty of the Piedmont district in Italy and it is the dried mushrooms that give it its European flavor.

    2 tbsp. dried mushrooms
    1 cup boiling water
    1 lb. veal, in one piece
    1 tsp. paprika
    2 tbsp. salad oil
    2 cans tomato sauce, 8-oz. each
    4 large onions, sliced
 ½ cup dry red wine
    1 tsp. basil
    1 garlic clove
 ½ tsp. sugar

Cover mushrooms with a cupful of boiling water and let them soak 1 hour.

Sprinkle veal with paprika and brown in the salad oil over medium heat. Reserving ¼ cup of tomato sauce, add remainder to pan with rest of ingredients, including mushroom water. Salt and pepper to taste and bring to a boil. Cover and simmer until meat is tender, about 1 hour.

Remove meat from sauce, let cool, then chop it finely with a sharp knife (if you put it through a meat chopper, you will lose too much juice). Return meat to sauce, add reserved tomato sauce and stir until well mixed and hot (do not boil). Taste for seasoning and serve over pasta of your choice. This sauce is even better made in advance and reheated. Also, it freezes well. Yield: 4 to 4½ cups.

Italian Cheese Loaf

This most versatile cheese loaf can be served hot or allowed to cool and sliced like bread, or, it can be cut into 2-inch squares and fried in butter or bacon fat and served with bacon.

   1 cup uncooked, short grain rice
   4 eggs
   6 tbsp. salad oil
   ½ tsp. basil
   ¼ cup minced parsley
   1 cup grated strong or mild cheese
      salt and pepper, to taste

Cook rice according to directions on package.

Beat 3 of the eggs with rotary beater, add salad oil, and beat well. Add the remaining ingredients and the cooked rice.

Oil a 6″ x 10″ loaf pan. Pour in mixture, spreading it evenly on top and cover with the well-beaten remaining egg. Bake in a 350°F. oven for 30 minutes. Good served with a tomato sauce. Serves 6.

Rice Parisien

In Paris in the spring, you will find this *riz blanc* served as a lunch specialty, garnished with watercress or a green salad.

   1 cup uncooked, long grain rice
   3 tbsp. butter
   ½ lb. cottage cheese
   ½ cup sour cream (commercial)
   4 green onions, finely minced
      minced parsley, to taste
      salt and pepper, to taste

Cook rice according to directions on package.

Melt the butter in a saucepan. Add the cooked rice, cottage cheese, sour cream, green onions, parsley, salt, and pepper. Stir together with a fork. Cover.

Cook over very low heat about 15 minutes or just enough to warm thoroughly, stirring once or twice during the cooking period. Serves 6.

Golden Rice Spinach Casserole

This is my favorite vegetable casserole with hot baked ham. It is also very good when topped with 4 to 6 sliced hard-cooked eggs and served as a main course.

   ⅓ cup salad oil
   1 tbsp. turmeric
   ¼ tsp. aniseed (optional)
   1 onion, chopped fine
   1 cup uncooked, short grain rice
   2 cups boiling water
   1¼ tsp. salt
   1 bag fresh spinach
   6 green onions, chopped fine
   ¼ cup fresh dill or parsley, chopped

Heat the salad oil, add the turmeric and aniseed. Stir quickly over high heat until they are quite hot. Add the onion and the rice, stir a few minutes or until well blended; lower the heat and cook 10 minutes, stirring often.

Add the boiling water and salt. Bring to a fast boil. Cover and simmer for 15 minutes.

Wash and chop the spinach rather coarsely. Slice the green onions; combine spinach, onion, and dill or parsley.

Make alternate layers of cooked rice and raw mixed greens in a buttered casserole. Salt and pepper each layer lightly. Top with a few dots of butter. Cover and bake for 30 minutes in a 350°F. oven. Serves 6.

Summer Rice Salad

Serve this light, colorful salad to replace a potato salad.

   1 cup uncooked, long grain rice
   2 carrots, peeled and grated
   ¼ cup green onions, chopped
   ¼ cup parsley, minced
   ¼ cup celery and leaves, finely chopped
   1 cup cooked green peas

Dressing:
½ tsp. salt
¼ tsp. pepper
¼ tsp. dry mustard
   pinch sugar
2 tbsp. cider or wine vinegar
4 tbsp. salad oil

Cook rice according to directions on package. Cool, and place in a bowl.

To the cooled rice add the carrots, green onions, parsley, celery and leaves, and green peas.

Blend together the salt, pepper, dry mustard, sugar, cider or wine vinegar, and salad oil. Pour over the rice, stir lightly with a fork until well mixed. Garnish with quartered hard-boiled eggs and tomato slices.

Wild Rice à la Ferguson

One cup of wild rice will make a main course for 6.

1 cup wild rice
3 tbsp. butter
1 small onion, minced
2 stalks celery, diced
½ cup fresh parsley, minced
¼ tsp. thyme
3 medium carrots, grated
½ lb. strong cheddar cheese, grated
1½ cups chicken stock
2 tbsp. butter, diced

Wash the rice under running water and spread on a towel to dry for 2 hours.

Melt the 3 tablespoons butter in a heavy frying pan. Brown the onion until tender. Remove from frying pan and add the dry wild rice to the remaining butter. Cook, stirring constantly, until a hazelnut fragrance emanates from the rice.

Mix together the celery, parsley, thyme, carrots, and browned onion. Butter a baking dish, fill with alternate layers of wild rice, vegetables, and grated cheese, until all the ingredients have been used up. Cover with the chicken stock. Dot with butter.

Cover and bake in a 350°F. oven for 1 hour.

Summer Cheese Soufflé

Since it's a fake soufflé, it waits for the guests — in fact, the longer it waits, the better the texture. Serve with a green salad for lunch or thinly sliced ham for dinner.

5 slices bread
   soft butter
½ to ¾ lb. sharp cheddar cheese, grated
4 eggs, beaten
2 cups milk
1 tsp. each dry mustard and Worcestershire sauce
½ tsp. each curry powder and salt

Butter each slice of bread generously and cut into cubes. In an ungreased one-quart casserole make alternating layers of the bread and cheese. Mix remaining ingredients and pour over bread, but do not mix. Cover and refrigerate for up to two days. To bake, place in a 350°F. oven for one hour. Serves 6.

Vegetables

7

Artichokes Barigoule

A classic of the French cuisine, simplified — easy to make — an elegant entrée for dinner, or a main course for lunch, served with thin slices of cold chicken.

> 6 large artichokes
> 2 medium-sized onions, thinly sliced
> 6 tbsp. olive oil
> 2 cloves garlic, chopped fine
> 1 tsp. salt
> ¼ tsp. pepper
> ¼ cup red wine vinegar
> ½ cup dry vermouth
> 1 can undiluted consommé
> 1 bay leaf
> ½ tsp. thyme

Cut off (with scissors) the top of each leaf, which will give a neat looking artichoke. Remove the small wilted leaves near the stem. Cut the stems to make a flat base. Open gently with the fingers, and invert the artichokes on a flat surface, one at a time, pressing down on bottom to open the leaves. Pull out the small white leaves and the chokes in the bottom — a bit awkward, but not difficult.

Brown the onions in the olive oil in a large shallow pan with a cover; stir in the garlic, salt, and pepper. Remove pan from heat.

Arrange artichokes, sitting on the onions, one next to the other. (this is what determines the size of pan). Cover and simmer over very low heat for 10 minutes. Then add the vinegar and vermouth. Boil, uncovered, over medium heat for 5 minutes. Add the undiluted consommé, bay leaf, and thyme. Cover with a J-cloth or a clean linen cloth, then cover. Bake one hour in a preheated 325°F. oven. Remove from oven and cool

without uncovering. Serve when cool or refrigerate for a day or so. To serve, place one artichoke on each plate. Stir the sauce and pour a generous spoonful on top.

Fresh Asparagus Casserole

I usually reserve the stems for this casserole and use the tips in a salad. It is perfect for a garden luncheon and, best of all, you can prepare it in the morning and refrigerate it uncooked until ready to bake.

> 2 tbsp. butter
> 1 small onion, minced
> 2 cups fresh mushrooms, sliced
> ½ tsp. curry powder
> 4 tbsp. flour
> 1 cup chicken broth
> 1 cup milk
> ½ tsp. salt
> 1 tsp. Worcestershire sauce
> 20 to 24 stalks cooked asparagus
> 2 hard-boiled eggs, sliced
> ½ cup bread cubes, toasted

Melt the butter in a large frying pan. Add the onion, stir over high heat for a few seconds, then add the sliced mushrooms and curry powder. Keep stirring for an additional minute or two.

Lower the heat, add the flour, and mix well. Mix in the chicken broth, then add the milk. Stir until smooth and creamy, then season with the salt and Worcestershire sauce.

Arrange the asparagus on the bottom of a generously buttered casserole. Top with the egg slices and pour the sauce over all. Sprinkle with the bread cubes and bake at 375°F. for 30 to 35 minutes. Serves 4 to 5.

Lemon Nutmeg Carrots

These carrots are one of my summer favorites. I cook the carrots, make the sauce, and refrigerate until needed. Then, in only a few minutes, the sauce and carrots can be combined and warmed just before dinner.

        12 young carrots
            a pinch of sugar
            salt, to taste
    1½ tsp. boiling water
        2 tbsp. butter
        1 tbsp. fresh lemon juice
    ⅛ tsp. nutmeg

Wash and scrape the carrots and place in a saucepan. Add a pinch of sugar, then pour boiling water on top. Cover and boil for 10 to 15 minutes, depending on the size of the carrots — keep them crisp. Drain. Salt to taste and refrigerate.

Combine the rest of the ingredients and refrigerate.

To serve, simmer the two together over low heat for 3 to 5 minutes; sprinkle with parsley. Serves 6.

Eggplant Tomato Casserole

All you need for an interesting lunch is this and parsleyed rice or a green salad.

    1½ to 2½-lb. eggplant
    1½ tsp. salt
        2 eggs, beaten
        2 tbsp. melted butter
        1 medium-sized onion, chopped
    ½ cup dry breadcrumbs
        1 tsp. basil or oregano
    ¼ tsp. pepper
        2 large tomatoes, thinly sliced
    ½ tsp. sugar
    ½ cup grated cheddar
    ¼ cup grated Parmesan

Peel and slice eggplant. Put in a saucepan with the salt and about 1 inch of boiling water. Cover and cook 10 minutes over high heat.

Drain thoroughly, then mash slices with a potato masher. Stir in eggs, butter, onion, breadcrumbs, and seasonings. Mix well.

Butter a shallow 1½-quart baking dish. Line bottom with half the tomato slices. Spoon egg-plant mixture on top and spread evenly. Arrange rest of tomato slices on top and sprinkle with sugar. Mix two cheeses and sprinkle over all. Bake in a 375°F. oven for about 45 minutes. Serves 6.

Irene's Creamed Mushrooms

The onion browns in a heavy metal pan without any fat. It is an intriguing way to deal with onions — they retain all their fine flavor with none of the harshness.

        1 onion, chopped fine
    ½ lb. fresh mushrooms, sliced
    ⅓ cup cold water
        2 tbsp. butter
        2 tbsp. flour
    ½ cup sour cream
            salt and pepper, to taste

Place the onion in a heavy metal frying pan without any fat. Cook over medium heat until lightly browned. Add the mushrooms, mix well, and stir together for a few minutes; add the water; simmer for 10 minutes.

In the meantime, brown the butter in a saucepan, add the flour and brown. Then add the liquid from the mushrooms and cook, while stirring, until creamy and smooth. Pour over the mushrooms. Blend together well and add the sour cream. Heat, but do not boil. Taste for seasoning and serve. Serves 4 to 6.

June-Fresh Green Peas

This is so good that I usually double the recipe and serve it as a main course for lunch, with crisp French bread and thin slices of Gouda cheese.

        3 tbsp. butter
        2 white onions, finely chopped
        1 medium head of lettuce
        2 to 3 lbs. unshelled green peas
    ½ tsp. sugar
        4 sprigs parsley

Melt the butter in a 300°F. frying pan. Add onions; cover and simmer until soft and transparent, but not brown. Reserve outer leaves of lettuce, shred rest, and place on onions. Shell peas, place over lettuce, and sprinkle with sugar.

Top with reserved lettuce leaves, cover, and lower heat to 200°F. Cook 25 to 30 minutes, depending on size of peas. When done, remove lettuce leaves. Season to taste, adding a piece of butter and a bit of lemon juice. Mix and garnish with parsley. Serves 6.

New Potatoes in Cucumber Sauce

To make ahead of time, cook and peel the potatoes, prepare the dressing; cover and keep both the potatoes and dressing at room temperature. They can then be combined in a matter of seconds before heating.

    18 to 24 small new potatoes
    5 to 6 green onions, finely chopped
    1 medium cucumber, unpeeled
      juice of 1 lemon
    1 tsp. salt
    ½ tsp. paprika
    4 tbsp. mayonnaise

Cook the whole potatoes in their skins, drain, and dry for a few seconds over the heat. Cool slightly and peel, cutting any large potatoes into thick slices. Mix in onions and set aside.

Grate the cucumber on a fine grater, removing all seeds. Place in top of a double boiler with remaining ingredients and stir over boiling water until well blended. Add potatoes and stir gently over simmering water until hot. Serves 10.

Best Mashed Potatoes

Over the years, I have tried many ways of preparing mashed potatoes. These are my winners — very smooth, white, and creamy. I prefer to pressure-cook my potatoes, but they can also be boiled.

    8 potatoes, peeled and halved
    4 tbsp. instant skim milk powder
    ½ to ¾ cup commercial sour cream
    ¼ tsp. savory
    1 green onion, minced (optional)
      salt and pepper, to taste

Boil the potatoes until tender. Drain and put pan back over heat until the potatoes are dry. Put potatoes through a potato ricer over the cooking pan, add the remainder of the ingredients, and beat until light and smooth.

Variations:
To serve with roast pork or sausages, add 2 cups of cooked mashed turnips to the above recipe; replace the savory with sage.

To serve with chicken, fish, or eggs, add 1½ cups cooked, mashed carrots to the above; replace savory with basil.

To serve with lamb, beef, or hamburger, add 1 cup of onion, fried in bacon fat and mixed with the savory, to the above recipe.

Barbecued Potatoes

Easy to make, perfect with all barbecued meats. Each variation gives the potatoes a different personality. The 7 oz. to 9 oz. sizes are the best.

Brush each potato with salad oil. Wrap each in a double thickness of heavy-duty foil. Bring edges together and fold over several times to seal firmly.

Cook toward back of grill, turning every 10 minutes until tender, for 40 to 55 minutes.

Variations:
Before baking top each potato with a bay leaf or a sprig of fresh summer savory, or half a clove of unpeeled garlic, or a thick slice of onion, or a slice of bacon.

Serve any of these combinations with a bowl of sour cream, fresh dill, and fresh chives. Superb!

Potato Pancakes

These are delicious with any pot roast or *daube*. Any leftover pancakes may be frozen.

    6 potatoes, peeled
    ¼ cup bread crumbs
    2 eggs, beaten
    1 onion, grated
      salt and pepper, to taste
    2 to 3 tbsp. bacon fat or lard

Grate peeled potatoes and keep in iced water to prevent them from turning black. When ready to make pancakes, drain potatoes and squeeze very dry in a towel (A terry towel is best). Combine potatoes with bread crumbs, beaten eggs, onion, salt, and pepper.

Heat fat in a frying pan and drop potato mixture, a spoonful at a time, into pan (as for pancakes). Brown on one side, turn and cook until brown on other side. Keep warm in oven. Serve with pickled red cabbage. Serves 6 to 8.

Elegant Colcannon

I call this dish Elegant Colcannon because I was inspired by the Irish cabbage and potato colcannon to create this combination with carrots. I sometimes substitute turnips for the carrots; at other times I add grated cheese, about ½ cup. It is excellent with roast turkey or chicken.

    4 to 6 carrots, peeled and cubed
    3 medium-sized potatoes, pared and cubed
    1 medium-sized onion, sliced
    ⅛ tsp. dried thyme or ½ tsp. dried basil
    3 tbsp. butter
       milk or water (about ⅔ cup)
    1 egg
    ¼ cup commercial sour cream
       salt and pepper
    ¼ cup chopped parsley

In a saucepan combine the carrots, potatoes, onion, thyme or basil, and 1 tablespoon of the butter. Add enough water or milk to cover 1 inch of the bottom. Cover and simmer until the vegetables are tender. This will take 10 to 15 minutes.

If you have a blender, pour in the drained vegetables and add just enough of the cooking liquid to make a thick purée; or make a purée by pressing the vegetables through a food mill or sieve.

To the hot purée, add the egg, sour cream, and the remaining butter. Add salt and pepper to taste. Whip over low heat until creamy and fluffy. Serve sprinkled with parsley. Serves 4 to 6.

Tomato Scallop

A tasty casserole that follows the weather, this scallop can be served hot on cold days, and cold on hot days. It is a good traveller, but you can also take the ingredients you need and quickly put them together at the cottage. Serve it with cold cuts or barbecued chicken.

    19 oz. can tomatoes
    1 onion, chopped
    1 tbsp. sugar
    ½ tsp. salt
    ¼ tsp. oregano
       dash rosemary
    1 cup bread, cut into ½-inch cubes
    ⅓ cup grated, mild cheddar cheese

Combine tomatoes, onion, sugar, and seasonings; top with bread cubes and grated cheese. Bake in 350°F. oven until bread cubes are browned, about 15 to 18 minutes. Serves 4 to 6.

Frittata

The best frittata is made in Genoa, with any combination of vegetables. I like it best when the vegetables are cooked in a shallow ceramic baking dish and the eggs are poured on top.

    1 tbsp. salad oil
    ½ tbsp. butter
    1 onion, thinly sliced
    1 green pepper, diced
    1 zucchini (small Italian squash)
    6 to 8 beet tops or spinach leaves, coarsely
       chopped or 1 peeled tomato, diced
    1 tbsp. water
    ½ tsp. sugar
    6 eggs
    3 tsp. cold water
       Parmesan cheese, grated

Heat together the oil and butter, add the onion, and cook until soft and lightly browned. Add the green pepper and stir for a few seconds. Slice the unpeeled zucchini and add to the green pepper mixture with the beet tops, spinach leaves, or tomatoes. Add the 1 tbsp. water and the sugar. Cover and simmer for 5 minutes over low heat.

Prepare the omelette mixture. Season vegetables with salt and pepper to taste, pour the omelette on top, and cook over low heat until set. Do not turn or fold. Slide the omelette on to a hot platter and serve with the grated cheese. Serves 6.

Eggplant Sauce — a subtle blend of eggplant, bacon, green pepper, and tomatoes, served on hot pasta and sprinkled with freshly grated cheese. Recipe on page 45.

Julienne of Vegetables

Since any combination of vegetables can be used, this is a very versatile dish. The important part is the cutting — it should be consistent so that all vegetables are the same size.

  5 medium carrots
  5 celery stalks
  2 medium onions
  2 parsnips or ½ a turnip
  1 leek (optional)
  4 tbsp. butter
  ½ tsp. thyme
  salt and pepper, to taste
  juice of ½ a lemon

Peel the vegetables and cut into match-like shreds. Melt butter in a saucepan just large enough to hold vegetables, add vegetables to pan with 2 tbsp. water, thyme, and salt and pepper to taste. Cover tightly and simmer over low heat for 20 to 35 minutes, or until tender. Add lemon juice and taste for seasoning. Serves 10.

Little Finnish Spinach Crêpes

Serve as an entrée with a spoonful of sour cream in the middle, topped with caviar or minced green onions, or, as a vegetable with roast chicken. Any leftovers can be slivered and used as garnish for hot consommé.

  ½ lb. fresh spinach
  1½ cups milk
  1 tsp. salt
  ⅛ tsp. nutmeg
  1 cup flour
  2 tbsp. melted butter
  2 to 3 eggs
  ½ tsp. sugar

Wash the spinach, pack into a saucepan (do not add water), cover, and cook over high heat for 3 to 4 minutes. Drain and chop finely; set aside.

Place all the remaining ingredients in a bowl.

I now use my Cuisinard food processor. I combine in the bowl with the blender knife all the ingredients, including the spinach (which in this case does not need to be chopped), I put the cover on and process mixture for 40 seconds or until smooth.

When using a bowl, stir with a whisk, until ingredients are well blended. Add the spinach; mix again.

To make the little crêpes: Use, if available, a cast iron *Plattar*, a Scandinavian 7-section pancake pan which makes the most delicate and dainty crêpes. Lacking this, use a heavy cast-iron frying pan. In either case, heat the pan; rub well with a buttered absorbent paper. Pour full teaspoons into each section or in the pan. Cook the same as pancakes, turning once.

They are at their best when served as soon as made, but if you have a microwave oven, set crêpes on a platter; cover with wax paper. When ready to serve, still covered with paper, microwave for 1 minute.

Gourmet Ideas for Vegetables

Of all foods, we abuse vegetables the most. We let the frozen ones steam their lives away. We let canned green peas turn into little more than yellow rubbery nuggets with no more flavor than warmed-over dumplings. Remember, there's more to it than "cook and drain."

Open a Can, Then 1-2-3

Do not drain the liquid from the cans down the sink — some of the vitamins, minerals, and soluble proteins have cooked into it. Instead, drain this tasty liquid into a saucepan, flavor with a pinch of herb, a bit of sugar, and a small piece of butter. Then, without covering it, boil rapidly for 5 minutes until the liquid has reduced to less than half of its original volume. Then, just before you are ready to serve them, add the vegetables and simmer (do not boil) for 3 minutes. All canned vegetables can be heated this way.

Frozen Vegetables Are Good—Sometimes Even Better

Frozen vegetables can be used in any way that fresh vegetables are — and you can cook them in even less water and in less time than specified on the package. If possible, use a heavy enameled cast-iron pan. In it melt 1 tbsp. butter, add ½ cup water, and a pinch of sugar or honey. (The latter compensates for the loss of some of the natural sugar which converts to starch after the vegetables are picked.) Place the frozen block of vegetables in the middle of the boiling water, butter, and sugar. Cover the pan, lower the heat, and simmer for 10 to 20 minutes, turning the vegetables once. Above all, do not overcook. There will be very little liquid left, and this can be evaporated by a few seconds of rapid boiling with the cover off. Then season or cream to taste.

I like to cook frozen squash and pumpkin in a double boiler with 2 tbsp. butter, a pinch of cinnamon or nutmeg, a large spoonful of sour cream, and, sometimes, for an added flourish, I pour in a few spoonfuls of brandy or rum. Cover, heat, beat, and eat — with delight.

Frozen corn on the cob I "steam boil" in ¼ cup milk sweetened with ½ tsp. sugar for 20 minutes. I use a heavy, covered saucepan, and keep the heat low. Salt tends to toughen the kernels.

For all other frozen vegetables I use an enameled cast-iron frying pan with a good cover, a bit of butter, and always a minimum of water. When cooked, the water has practically evaporated and the vegetables are beautifully seasoned with the butter. Sometimes, for a creamed effect, I add a large spoonful of sour cream just before serving. For a classical Greek effect, I substitute olive oil for the butter and add fresh lemon juice just before serving. It is good both for flavor and digestion.

Season Vegetables Imaginatively

One of our greatest mistakes is to take vegetables for granted. When it comes to serving them, too many cooks expect them to somehow look after themselves. Even the humblest vegetables should be treated with respect and affection. Those that you buy frozen or canned have already had a good start. All you have to do with them is to follow a few basic rules:

To sweet-tasting vegetables, such as cabbage and greens add a little lemon or lime juice, or a pinch of rosemary, or a few whole cloves, or a sprinkling of curry.

To carrots, potatoes or turnips add minced chives or parsley or coarsely ground black pepper, or a pinch of thyme.

To spinach add a little mace or nutmeg, or a dash of tarragon vinegar, or a bit of crushed or fried garlic, or sour cream and sesame seeds.

To beets add 2 whole cloves while cooking, or serve with sour cream or minced green onions. Also good with a dash of malt vinegar or a pinch of fresh dill or dill seeds.

To green peas or wax beans add the classic touch of finely chopped mint while cooking, or a pinch of summer savory, or crisp bacon when ready to serve, or, add a dash of curry.

Any vegetable can be the highlight of a meal with the addition of a little lemon juice, chutney, vinaigrette* or salad dressing. Whichever one you use, add it just before serving.

*Vinaigrette sauce is a spiced vinegar, boiled down, and mixed with some white or red wine and some finely cut green onions, tarragon, parsley, and a few drops of lemon juice. Finely cut capers, without their vinegar, can also be added.

Quick Tricks with Fresh Vegetables

Lettuce with a Continental Air: Serve a wedge of lettuce with sardines perched on it, garnished with hard-boiled eggs and lemon wedges. No dressing. Try vegetable salt (buy at health food shop) and freshly ground pepper with lemon, which give a dew-fresh feeling. Add hot bread and large bowl of berries.

Salad Luncheon: Make individual bowls of crisp lettuce (try romaine), quartered and seeded tomatoes, cottage cheese, and lots of crisp bacon broken up into small pieces. Buy, get from your garden, or beg from a neighbor, a handful of fresh herbs (basil, marjoram, dill, or tarragon) and sprinkle on salad. Toss with French dressing. Serve with crackers, crisped in oven just before serving. Finish with old-fashioned gingerbread à la mode (made from cake-mix).

Lots of Tomatoes: This is my favorite with all barbecues. For 6 people — quarter 12 unpeeled tomatoes, put them skin side down in large frying pan. Add 2 diced onions. Dot generously with butter, sprinkle with good dose of brown sugar or maple sugar, then cook, uncovered, over a really slow fire for a good 1½ hours. Never stir, just shake pan occasionally. Tomatoes become dark brown and luscious! Yes, you can cook them on the barbecue away from the intense heat, in the same frying pan.

Green Peas à la Parisienne: Melt 1 tbsp. butter, add enough shredded lettuce to cover bottom of saucepan, top with few slivers of onion, a pinch of sugar, and the well-drained canned green peas. No salt, please. Cover and simmer 10 minutes.

Canned Beets the Dutch Way: Drain 1 can diced beets, add them to 2 minced onions lightly browned in butter, with 1 tbsp. vinegar, a pinch of sugar, salt, and pepper. Heat and serve.

Four Rules for Tasty Vegetables

1. Perhaps the strictest rule in vegetable cookery is this: Always cook your vegetables in the shortest time possible. The surest way to have unattractive and flavorless vegetables is to let them cook too long.

2. You'll find that the not-so-fresh vegetables of fall and winter are improved by sprinkling a pinch of sugar over them before cooking. A little sugar also helps canned and frozen vegetables at all seasons.

3. To clean vegetables, simply scrub them under warm water. Don't peel them — unless the skin is tough or too uneven to clean thoroughly — because most of the nutritive value is lost with the peelings.

4. Never salt vegetables until just before serving. Salt draws out moisture, and if it is added at the beginning of the cooking, it drains away the vitamins, minerals, sugars — all the flavor and nutritive value.

Salads

8

Portuguese Gazpacho

Quite different from the usual gazpacho. Perfect to serve as a cold salad with a summer barbecue.

2 cucumbers, diced
4 tomatoes, diced
6 green onions, chopped fine
¼ cup parsley, minced
½ tsp. salt
¼ tsp. pepper
1 tsp. sugar
juice 1 lemon
¼ cup oil
4 slices toasted bread, diced
½ head lettuce

Combine all the ingredients except the lettuce. Refrigerate until ready to serve. Will keep 2 to 3 days refrigerated.

To serve, add lettuce. Taste for seasoning. Serves 6.

Cucumber Mizeria

Summer should not go by without fresh cucumbers in this tasty, creamy sauce being served at least once. This recipe is Ukrainian.

3 medium cucumbers
1 tsp. salt
4 to 5 chopped green onions
1 tbsp. minced fresh dill
3 tbsp. white vinegar
½ tsp. salt
½ tsp. sugar
¼ tsp. pepper
¼ cup sour cream

Peel the cucumbers; if they are young and freshly gathered, just wash them. Peeled or unpeeled, run a fork down their length to make parallel grooves which create an attractive scalloped edge. Then slice as thinly as possible.

Transfer to a dish; sprinkle with the salt and let stand for 15 minutes. Drain, press out the water that has accumulated, and place the slices in the serving bowl.

Add the onions, dill, vinegar, salt, sugar, and pepper. Toss well and refrigerate for 1 hour, or, just let stand for 5 minutes. Spread the sour cream on top just before serving. A sprig of dill placed on top of the sour cream looks pretty. Serves 4.

Dutch Coleslaw

If you are going to have a harvest party, consider serving a large, cold boiled ham, hot boiled potatoes, and this fine Dutch Coleslaw. A big jar of good mustard, apple dumplings, and cider will make the meal perfect.

4 to 5 cups thinly sliced cabbage
2 diced celery stalks
2 thinly sliced onions
4 grated carrots, cut into medium shreds
2 tbsp. sugar
½ cup rich cream
2 tbsp. cider vinegar
½ to 1 tsp. salt
¼ tsp. pepper.
¼ cup minced, fresh parsley

Combine the cabbage, celery, onions, and carrots. Place them in a large bowl and completely cover with ice water. Refrigerate for 1 hour, then drain thoroughly.

Combine the sugar, cream, vinegar, salt, and pepper (the vinegar will thicken the cream). Pour over the vegetables when ready to serve and toss very well. Sprinkle the minced parsley on top. Serves 6.

Old-Fashioned Potato Salad

This potato salad keeps very well, and is most tasty. The cooked dressing is my grandmère's. My mother taught me how to make the salad; the oil dressing is my recipe.

> **5 to 6 cups cooked potatoes, diced**
> **1 tsp. salt**
> **¼ tsp. pepper, freshly ground**
> **¼ tsp. dry mustard**
>   **generous pinch tarragon**
>   **pinch garlic powder (optional)**
> **1 tbsp. fresh lemon juice**
> **3 tbsp. salad oil**
> **1 cup celery, diced**
>   **crisp lettuce or watercress**

Place the diced potatoes in a large bowl. Shake the salt, pepper, dry mustard, tarragon, garlic powder, lemon juice, and salad oil together in a bottle.

Pour mixture over the potatoes, toss gently, and cover the bowl. Let stand for 2 hours but do not refrigerate.

When ready to serve, add the celery and ½ cup or so of Grandmère's Cooked Dressing (page 64). Mix lightly and serve in a nest of lettuce or watercress. Serves 6 to 8.

Potato Civette

A fantastic potato salad created by a French epicure friend of mine who says it refreshes the palate and enhances the fineness of the accompanying meat. I can vouch for the truth of this. Serve it in a black ebony bowl or in gleaming cut glass as the French do.

> **16 to 20 small potatoes (all the same size)**
> **¼ cup chives or green onion tops, chopped fine**
> **1 tsp. sugar**
> **¼ tsp. freshly ground pepper**
> **½ tsp. salt**
> **2 tbsp. olive oil**
>   **juice of 2 lemons**

Peel a little band, about an inch wide, around the middle of each scrubbed potato.

Place the potatoes in a steamer (a sort of double boiler with the bottom of its top piece perforated) or in a sieve or colander that can rest on the rim of a pot of boiling water, but well above the water, as the potatoes are steamed, not boiled. Cover pan.

Steam 20 to 30 minutes or until potatoes are tender. Turn on to a folded cloth and let them cool until they can be handled, then remove peel which almost comes off by itself.

Prepare the dressing while the potatoes cool. In a mortar or in a bowl place the chives or green onions, sugar, pepper, and salt. Crush this to a paste with the pestle or a wooden spoon, slowly adding the oil and lemon juice alternately. Then stir for about 5 minutes until mixture becomes slightly creamy. Pour over the potatoes; stir until well mixed. The potatoes will take on a lime green color. Arrange in serving dish. Sprinkle lightly with paprika. Cover with wax paper and keep at room temperature until ready to use. Serves 8.

French Potato Salad

A true continental potato salad with a personality!

> **4 cups (about 6 medium) uncooked potatoes, peeled and sliced ¼-inch thick**
> **2 tbsp. chicken stock, fresh, canned, or from cubes**
> **1 tsp. salt**
> **½ tsp. dry English mustard**
> **½ tsp. French Dijon mustard**
> **¼ tsp. freshly ground pepper**
> **2 tbsp. wine or cider vinegar**
> **4 tbsp. peanut or olive oil**
> **2 tbsp. minced green onion**
> **1 tbsp. parsley, chopped fine**

Drop the potato slices into rapidly boiling salted water. Use large enough pan so potatoes are not all stuck together. Cook over high heat until tender but not soft. Drain and dry for a few seconds over medium heat. Then, while they are still hot, place in a large mixing bowl. Pour the chicken stock over them. Stir gently for a few seconds so the stock is absorbed. In a bowl beat the salt, mustards, pepper, vinegar, and the oil; add the green onions and parsley. Pour over the potatoes. Blend well, cover, and serve at room temperature. If you wish to prepare 6 to 12 hours before serving, take salad out of refrigerator 2 hours before serving to take the chill off. Serves 6.

Tyrolian Tomatoes

Prepare this colorful cooked salad a day or so ahead of time. Surrounded with crisp watercress, it looks very dramatic presented in individual French porcelain ramekins or a smart Copenhagen blue serving dish.

  ½ lb. fresh mushrooms (see below)
  4 tbsp. olive oil
  1 large onion, finely chopped
  2 garlic cloves, finely chopped
  ¼ cup vinegar (red wine or cider)
  1 tsp. sugar
  4 to 6 peeled tomatoes, chopped
  ¼ tsp. thyme
  1 crushed bay leaf
  2 tbsp. finely chopped parsley

Use button mushrooms if possible, removing stems and leaving caps whole. If not available, remove stems from ordinary mushrooms and slice caps. Heat 3 tablespoons of the oil in a frying pan, stir mushroom caps over high heat for 3 minutes, and set aside.

Heat remaining oil in a saucepan; add onion, garlic; stir constantly over medium heat until lightly browned. Add vinegar, sugar, and boil uncovered over medium heat until reduced by half. Add tomatoes, thyme, bay leaf, parsley, and simmer uncovered over low heat for 30 minutes.

Add mushrooms, stir thoroughly, and pour into a dish. Let cool, and, when tepid, add salt and pepper to taste. Cover and refrigerate until needed. I fill my ramekins in the morning and refrigerate them until 1 hour before serving. Serves 4 to 6.

Tomato-Cucumber Salad

My family's favorite whenever we have an outdoor charcoal-broiled feast.

  4 tomatoes, sliced
  ¼ cup salad oil
  ¼ cup cider or red wine vinegar
  1 tbsp. parsley, chopped
    dill, fresh or dried, to taste
  3 green onions, finely chopped
    small head of lettuce
  2 cucumbers, peeled and sliced
    salt and pepper, to taste

Place the tomatoes in a bowl with the oil,

vinegar, parsley, dill, and onions. Refrigerate 1 to 2 hours. When ready to serve, shred the lettuce as you would a cabbage, add to tomatoes with the cucumbers, salt, and pepper. Toss lightly until well blended. Serves 4.

Orange and Pimiento Salad

A wonderfully colorful salad, this teams a fruit and vegetable in an unusual combination.

  6 large oranges
  6 sweet red peppers
  5 tbsp. salad oil
  3 tbsp. wine vinegar
  1 tsp. Dijon mustard
    salt, to taste

Place oranges in a large bowl of boiling water; leave 15 minutes, then drain. Peel when cool enough, removing all cellulose (the white inner skin) and slice thinly.

Remove cores, seeds, and membranes from washed peppers and cut into julienne strips. Beat together remaining ingredients.

Place alternate layers of oranges and peppers in a bowl, sprinkling each layer with the dressing. Chill, and, just before serving, stir gently. Serves 6.

Golden Eggs Mayonnaise

This is the English version of the French Eggs Mimosa. It makes an elegant, tasty luncheon served with garlic bread sticks.

  4 tbsp. butter
  1 tbsp. oil
  2 tbsp. curry powder
  8 hard boiled eggs
  1 cup mayonnaise
  3 tbsp. chopped chutney
  1 head of lettuce
  ½ cup chopped olives

Heat the butter and oil in a saucepan over medium heat. Stir in curry powder until well blended. Add peeled whole eggs and turn constantly over low heat 10 minutes to coat them thoroughly. Remove to a plate with a slotted spoon, cover, and cool (do not refrigerate).

To serve, mix the mayonnaise with chutney; cut eggs in half. Make a nest of lettuce in salad bowl, add eggs, then pour mayonnaise over to coat them. Sprinkle chopped olives around the mayonnaise. Serves 4-6.

9

Dressings, Sauces, and Garnishes

Tartar Sauce

This sauce is the classic accompaniment for fried or baked fish, but it is also good with fried mushrooms.

1 cup mayonnaise
2 tbsp. finely chopped sour pickles
1 tbsp. capers
1 small onion, finely chopped
3 sprigs parsley, chopped

Mix ingredients and chill for at least 3 hours — excellent in a cup of crisp lettuce leaves. Yield: 1 cup.

Tomato Concassé

Despite the name, this sauce is not French, but a specialty of Sweden. It is excellent on fresh trout or salmon, rice, or an omelet.

6 to 8 tomatoes
1 small onion, finely chopped
2 tbsp. salad oil
1 crushed clove garlic
1 tbsp. finely chopped parsley
¼ tsp. each tarragon and fresh dill or dill seeds
½ tsp. sugar or honey

Pour boiling water over the tomatoes in a bowl, let stand 3 minutes, then peel and cut in half. Discard squeezed juice and seeds, and chop tomatoes coarsely.

Fry onion in oil until golden brown here and there. Mix in well the tomatoes and remaining ingredients, cover, and simmer over low heat for 20 to 25 minutes (do not boil or overcook, it must simmer slowly). Season to taste. Serves 4.

Fresh Onion Cucumber Relish

This relish takes but a minute to make and goes so well with a ham loaf or fish.

2 sweet onions, thinly sliced
1 peeled cucumber, thinly sliced
3 tbsp. cider vinegar
⅓ cup peanut oil
1 tsp. salt
¼ cup minced parsley

Place all the ingredients in a screw-top jar. Cover and give it a few shakes. Let stand covered from 2 days to 3 weeks. Shake well before serving. This relish loses its crispness if not kept cool, but does not spoil or lose its flavor.

Citrus Dressing for Roast Pork

This citrus dressing is the best I know of for pork. It can be used for a crown roast of pork, or for a boned leg of pork. To serve with a roast loin of pork, bake the dressing separately.

¼ cup butter
1 cup diced celery
1 large onion, diced
2 medium-size apples, peeled and chopped
6 cups diced bread
1 tsp. ground sage
¼ tsp. ground marjoram
1 can (8 oz.) whole cranberry sauce
¼ cup brown sugar
1 tsp. salt
grated rind of 1 orange
½ cup fresh orange juice

Melt the butter in a frying pan and add celery, onion, and apples. Stir over medium-low heat until softened, but do not brown. Add diced bread, sage, and marjoram. In a saucepan combine the cranberry sauce, brown sugar, salt, and orange rind. Stir together over low heat until the sugar has dissolved. Add to the bread mixture. Add the orange juice gradually, continuing to mix until the bread is moist. It is now ready to use as a stuffing for any type of roast pork.

To bake separately, put in a baking dish and bake, covered, at 350°F. for 1 hour.

My Applesauce for Meat

Serve hot with roast pork, ham, duck, goose, or sausages.

2 lbs. apples, peeled, quartered, and cored
2 tbsp. water
2 whole cloves
2 tbsp. sugar
3 tbsp. butter
juice and grated rind of ½ a lemon

Combine apples, water, cloves, and sugar in a saucepan. Cover and simmer over low heat until apples are soft. Remove cloves. Add butter, lemon juice and rind, and whisk until smooth. Serve hot. Yield: 1 pint.

Grandmère's Cooked Dressing

Covered and refrigerated, this dressing will keep for 4 to 8 weeks in a glass jar. It goes well with all types of vegetable salads.

3 tbsp. butter
2 tbsp. all-purpose flour
1½ tsp. salt
1 tsp. dry mustard
1 tbsp. sugar
sprinkling of mace or nutmeg
1¼ cups milk or cream
2 egg yolks
⅓ cup cider vinegar
½ onion, peeled and sliced

Melt the butter in a heavy metal saucepan. Mix in the flour, salt, mustard, sugar, and mace or nutmeg. Blend completely into the butter and add 1 cup of the milk or cream. Cook over low heat, stirring most of the time, until mixture is slightly thickened and creamy.

Beat the remaining ¼ cup of milk or cream together with the egg yolks. Stir into the hot mixture, beating well after each addition. When well mixed, add the remaining ingredients (be sure to use cider vinegar only). Simmer over low heat until thickened. Cool, remove the onion slices, and refrigerate. Yield: 1½ cups.

Lemon Dressing

This is an excellent basic dressing for a green salad. A teaspoon of chopped fresh herbs, when available, really enhances it: basil, tarragon, chives, parsley, coriander, marjoram, or thyme taste best.

⅔ cup salad oil
½ cup fresh lemon juice
¼ tsp. each sugar and dry mustard
¼ tsp. freshly ground black pepper
1 whole garlic clove
1 tsp. salt

Place all the ingredients in a screw-top jar and shake vigorously until blended. Remove garlic after a few days; the dressing will keep about a month in a cool place (preferably not the refrigerator). Yield: 1 cup.

Blender Mustard Hollandaise

Use your blender and you will make perfect hollandaise. If you do not have a blender, follow your favorite recipe and add the teaspoon of mustard after the sauce has cooked.

4 egg yolks
2 tbsp. fresh lemon juice
1 cup (½ lb.) butter
4 tsp. very hot water
½ tsp. salt
few drops of Tabasco
1 tsp. Dijon mustard

Combine the egg yolks and lemon juice in blender, cover, and blend for 10 seconds at high speed. Melt butter until it bubbles. Gradually add hot water to yolks while blending at medium speed, then add hot butter in a slow, steady stream.

Turn off blender, add remaining ingredients, cover, and blend at high speed for 30 seconds. Pour into a serving dish, cover, and keep at room temperature. It is best to make it on the day that it is to be used rather than the day before. Yield: 2 cups.

Minty Fruit Salad Dressing

This dressing adds a touch of class to any fruit salad. Serve with half a papaya, stuffed with grapefruit — a creation "digne d'un chef."

⅓ cup fresh orange juice
1 tbsp. sugar
2 tsp. cornstarch
¼ tsp. salt
1 egg, lightly beaten
grated peel of ½ an orange, ½ a lemon
2 tbsp. fresh lemon juice
⅓ cup commercial sour cream
1 tsp. to 1 tbsp. finely chopped fresh mint

Combine orange juice, sugar, cornstarch, and salt in a saucepan, and stir over medium heat until smooth and transparent, stirring constantly, until it comes to a boil.

Beat the egg with the orange and lemon rind and lemon juice. While stirring, add to creamy mixture. Cook a minute or two, stirring briskly. Cool. Then add the sour cream and fresh mint. Keep covered and refrigerated. Yield: 1 cup.

Apricot Dressing for Fruit Salad

I like this so much that every season I freeze some mashed fresh apricots with sugar and lime juice. In the winter, I thaw the mixture and add the rest of the ingredients to make the dressing.

6 to 8 very ripe apricots (about 1 cup mashed)
juice of 1 fresh lime
3 tbsp. sugar
2 tbsp. mayonnaise
1 cup heavy cream, whipped
few drops yellow coloring

Halve the apricots and remove pits. Blend in a blender for 3 seconds, or force through a sieve to make a purée. Add the lime juice and sugar; stir until well blended. (If you want to freeze the

mixture, do it at this point.) Add the mayonnaise and fold mixture into the whipped cream. Color to taste.

Pile on fruit salad. For a sophisticated garnish, top with a few green pistachio nuts. Yield: 2½ cups.

Quick Tricks with Sauces

English Cucumber Sauce: Are you serving a fabulous fresh boiled salmon, cold or hot? Try my cucumber sauce, that I found in England years ago. Have all ingredients very cold before you start. Peel and grate 1 cucumber. Whip ½ cup cream, add very slowly 2 tablespoons tarragon vinegar, gradually beating all the time. Season. Just before serving, mix in grated cucumber.

Superb Gravy and Vegetables: All in one, for your roast lamb or beef. Remove roast from drippings, but do not remove any of the fat. Place pan over direct heat. Add 1 can undiluted consommé, 1 box frozen peas (not thawed out), and, either 1 tablespoon tomato paste, or, 1 tablespoon rye or Scotch. Stir over medium heat until peas are tender, about 8 to 10 minutes.

Quick Tricks with Sour Cream

I love sour cream (the commercial type) and here are a few of my favorite methods of serving it:

Call it Devonshire Cream, and pour it over berries, sprinkled with maple sugar.

Add a large, large, spoonful to your veal or chicken gravy; blend, but do not boil.

Top your cold soup with it, sprinkle with chives.

Melt a package of chocolate chips, pour while hot over ½ cup sour cream. Stir. It makes a divine ice cream sauce or sponge cake topping. Or, you can serve it with pears.

Perfect dressing for summer vegetable salad.

A dream on cucumbers. To 1 cup sour cream, add 1 teaspoon salt, 2 tablespoons tarragon vinegar (or use what you have), 1 teaspoon dry mustard, 1 teaspoon sugar, ½ teaspoon paprika.

Herbs

10

Herbs enhance, very often improve, and certainly vary the flavor of our daily foods. But use them sparingly — a heavy hand can ruin a dish.

When using herbs for the first time, experiment cautiously. But, since the quantities given in recipes are only suggestions, you can ignore the directions — simply add a pinch, let it simmer a few minutes, then taste and add another pinch.

Using all the available herbs would only confuse and even discourage the beginner, so become thoroughly acquainted with the nine basic ones first — bay leaves, thyme, basil, marjoram, mint, sage, summer savory, parsley, and chives.

Bay Leaves are sold dried and should be judged by their color — the greener the better. A bay leaf or two, combined with a few thin slices of unpeeled lemon enhances a cut-up chicken while it cooks slowly in butter, or, is baked in the oven. When in doubt about which herb to use, add a bay leaf — the flavor pleases everyone.

Thyme is one of the oldest herbs. It has a sweet, penetrating, and pleasing aroma but, because of this, it must be used with discretion. A small pinch will give a better flavor to all types of meats, vegetables, and soups. For example, with parsley, flavor a bread stuffing for chicken or fish; use in the flour to roll fish fillets before frying; and for veal dishes of all kinds. A touch of thyme enhances a clam chowder, home-made or canned. A good measure for cooked greens, a salad, or a sauce is ¼ tsp. of thyme for each 1 tsp. of grated lemon peel.

Basil is a pleasantly scented and lively herb. It is popular in Italian cuisine and can always be used with pasta and all Italian sauces. It is equally successful with tomato dishes, potatoes, cucumbers, seafood, and, especially, lamb. A pinch of basil added to eggs while they are being prepared makes beautiful scrambled eggs. A good salad to serve with steak is sliced tomatoes, simply sprinkled with a dash of sugar, a lot of freshly ground pepper, and basil to taste. Try frying mushrooms with a chopped green onion, then adding salt, pepper, and basil.

Chives are not always available, so grow them in your garden. They are the most delicate member of the onion family and, except for desserts, can add a happy touch to any dish you prepare. Many people who do not like the tang and flavor of onion enjoy the mild, pleasant taste of fresh chives. They are delicious blended into creamed cheese, perfect in an omelette, and are at home sprinkled on any green salad.

A hard-boiled egg and white sauce is especially elegant with fresh chives, as are deviled eggs when chives are blended into the yolks.

Marjoram is an herb of the mint family, and the very popular oregano is frequently called wild marjoram. Their similar flavor makes them interchangeable. Marjoram is versatile and enhances the flavor of meats, soups, stuffings, stews, and many vegetables. For instance, make little pockets in a roast of pork and stuff them with some marjoram and a bit of garlic. Brown pork chops on one side, turn, sprinkle with pepper and a generous amount of marjoram. Add 1 tsp. of marjoram to your favorite meat loaf mixture, and also add it to your favorite spaghetti sauce, combined with an equal quantity of basil.

If you use canned spaghetti sauce, add a pinch of basil and marjoram and a bit of lemon peel.

Mint and cucumber have a great affinity; and fresh, frozen, or canned green peas enjoy being flavored with it, too. In India, they make a fresh mint chutney to eat with curry. Simply combine 2 cups of chopped mint leaves, 2 chopped green onions, 3 tbsp. of fresh lemon juice, ½ tsp. of salt, 1 tbsp. of sugar, ⅛ or ¼ tsp. of cayenne. It will keep for several days if it is stored, covered, in the refrigerator.

Canteloupe, blueberries, and raspberries are very fond of mint. For each 1 qt. of cleaned fruit, mix ½ cup of sugar with finely chopped fresh mint to taste. Chopped fresh mint is also good sprinkled in lemon or lime sherbet.

To make mint tea, simply place the fresh or dried mint in a teaspoon, hold it carefully over a glass, and pour boiling water on top. Let it stand for 5 minutes, sweeten to taste, and serve hot or cold. If you have made it too strong, dilute with boiling water.

Parsley is surely the most familiar herb of all. It is too bad that so many people use it only as a garnish. Parsley is most frequently chopped to flavor and color sauces, or to sprinkle on potatoes, yet it can also be very good when used in large quantities.

My favorite hamburger mix is ½ lb. of ground beef combined with ½ lb. of ground pork, salt and pepper to taste, 1 egg, and 1 cup, yes, a whole cup, of chopped fresh parsley. Shake and broil. Try rolling boiled beets in butter and lots of chopped parsley; one-quarter cup of it added to ½ cup of butter, with fresh chives to taste, is a perfect butter for hot bread.

To me, the crowning glory of parsley is the way the Scandinavians use it to stuff a chicken. Brush the inside of the bird with 1 tsp. of salt mixed with 2 tsp. of cider vinegar or fresh lemon juice. Then stuff as much fresh parsley as you can into the cavity. Tie up and roast the chicken as usual. Make a sauce by adding half a cup of chopped parsley to the pan juices.

Sage has an affinity for all game birds, as well as pork and veal, but, since it is a powerful, assertive herb, go easy — just a little will give a tang to braised meat, croquettes, and stews. There is a great deal of difference in the flavor of fresh and dried sage. Both are good, but the fresh is less powerful, so experiment. Combine 2 cups of fresh bread crumbs, 1 cup of sausage meat, 1 cup of grated unpeeled apples, a bit of chopped onion, and ½ tsp. of sage. Salt to taste, and you have a good stuffing for wild or domestic duck. Triple the recipe for a goose. Add ½ to 1 tsp. of sage to your next meat and tomato macaroni, and sprinkle a bit on your sausages when they are almost cooked. Sprinkle sage over fried onions; it also goes well with lima beans. Combine equal amounts of sage, thyme, and marjoram. Keep in an airtight jar and use some when making hot biscuits or homemade bread or cornbread.

Savory is often a confusing term. Winter savory, a perennial, has a more pungent smell, but most dried savory on sale in our markets is the summer type, an annual which is much milder in flavor. Savory is distinctly aromatic, but not as powerful as sage. Savory and bay leaf could be the only two seasonings in your kitchen, because, combined or alone, they can satisfactorily flavor almost any food. In Germany and Holland, savory is always used with fresh green or wax beans, or with dried beans. With the fresh, sprinkle a pinch on top before boiling. Add ½ tsp. savory to 1 to 2 cups of white sauce for creamed cabbage. Mix fine bread crumbs, lemon peel, and savory to coat fish or veal scallops. Add a pinch to the horseradish sauce to be served with boiled beef, and use it to flavor hash and split pea soup.

Quick Breads

11

Butter Crumb Gingerbread

This is a delicious, crunchy, butter-topped ginger-bread. It keeps very well. I found this recipe in a 1935 English magazine, and to this day I bake it with the same excellent results.

    2 cups cake flour or 1⅔ cups all-purpose flour
    1 tsp. baking soda
    1 cup sugar
    1 tsp. cinnamon
    2 tsp. ginger
    ¼ tsp. salt
    ½ cup shortening or soft chicken fat
    2 tbsp. molasses
    1 egg
    1 cup buttermilk
Topping:
    2 tbsp. butter, very soft
    1 tbsp. flour
    4 tbsp. sugar
    ½ tsp. cinnamon or ginger

Sift together, three times, the flour, soda, sugar, cinnamon, ginger, and salt. Cut in the shortening or chicken fat until a fine crumb mixture is obtained. Beat the molasses and egg together well and add to the crumb mixture. Add the buttermilk, mix well, and pour into a greased 8 x 8 x 2 inch pan.

For the topping, spread the very soft butter lightly over the top. Mix together the flour, sugar, cinnamon, or ginger and sprinkle on top of the buttered batter. Bake at 350°F. for 45 minutes.

Old-Fashioned Hot Gingerbread

This may be baked ahead of time and warmed up at 300°F. Our grandmothers used to call it soft gingerbread — the cookie was the snap or hard gingerbread — and it is delicious served with beaten butter and green applesauce or stewed rhubarb.

    ½ cup sugar
    ½ cup molasses or English treacle
    ¼ cup melted butter or bacon fat
    2¼ cups all-purpose flour
    1 cup hot water minus 2 tbsp. (⅞ cup)
    ½ to 1 tsp. ginger
    1 tsp. baking soda

Mix the sugar, molasses or treacle, and melted butter or bacon fat. Add the flour and stir until thoroughly mixed.

Mix the hot water, ginger, and baking soda. Add all at once to the flour mixture. Mix enough to blend everything together.

Pour the batter into a well-buttered 8 x 8 x 2 inch pan. (If you use a Pyrex or pyroceram dish, it will not have to be unmolded.) Bake at 350°F. for 30 to 35 minutes or until done.

Butter-Dipped Biscuits

These are rich and relatively expensive but utterly scrumptious when served piping hot, topped with a cold berry compote. This recipe can easily be cut in half.

    1 cup butter or margarine
    4 cups all-purpose flour
    1 tsp. salt
    ½ cup sugar
    5 tsp. baking powder
    4 large eggs
    1 cup milk

Put the butter in a jelly roll pan and warm in a 450°F. oven until melted. Sift together the flour, salt, sugar, and baking powder. Stir together the eggs and milk. Pour egg mixture over the dry ingredients all at once, and stir until blended. Turn dough on to a generously floured board and knead gently with the tips of fingers, just enough to form into a ball. Pat the dough to a thickness of half an inch.

Cut into fingers, rounds, or diamonds in the size you prefer. Roll both sides of the biscuits in the melted butter, then place them in any remaining melted butter in the pan, and bake in a 450°F. oven for 15 to 18 minutes or until brown.

Top with cold berries and serve. Yield 16 to 18 2-inch biscuits.

Apple Cheese Bread

Apple and sharp cheddar combine to give a tangy and sweet flavor to this quick bread. I always keep some frozen for emergencies. Thirty minutes in a 325°F. oven will thaw it, ready to be served for tea or breakfast with butter and marmalade.

  ½ cup shortening
  ⅔ cup sugar
   2 eggs, beaten
1½ cups grated, unpeeled apples
  ½ cup grated, sharp cheddar cheese
  ¼ cup chopped walnuts
   2 cups all-purpose flour
1½ tsp. baking powder
  ½ tsp. each soda and salt

Cream shortening and sugar, add eggs, and mix well. Add apples, cheese, and nuts; blend the whole together. Add sifted dry ingredients and mix lightly. Bake in a well-greased 9 x 5 inch loaf pan in a 350°F. oven 50 to 60 minutes.

Cottage Cheese Biscuits

Lightly textured inside, crisp and crusty on top, these biscuits can be served either for breakfast, with fruit, salad, or soup, or with the main course instead of bread.

  1 egg, lightly beaten
  3 tbsp. milk
  1 cup cottage cheese, any kind
  2 tbsp. butter, melted
  2 scant cups all-purpose flour
  4 tsp. baking powder
  1 tsp. salt
  ¼ cup fresh parsley, minced

Preheat the oven to 450°F. Mix the egg, milk, cottage cheese, and butter thoroughly.

Stir together the flour, baking powder, salt, and parsley. Add to the first mixture and blend with the fingertips. If necessary, add more milk, a few drops at a time, to make the dough hold together.

Turn on to a floured board and knead for 30 seconds. Pat into a shape ½-inch thick, then cut into 18 squares.

Place on a greased baking sheet and bake for about 12 minutes or until golden brown.

Scotch Tea Cakes

Quick, easy, delicious. They keep well — if you can keep them.

  ½ cup unsalted butter
  1 cup dark brown sugar
  2 cups rolled oatmeal
  ¼ tsp. salt
  1 tsp. baking powder
  ½ cup chocolate chips
  ¼ cup chopped walnuts
  ⅛ tsp. caraway or anise seeds

Combine the butter and brown sugar in saucepan. Cook and stir over low heat, until butter melts. Remove from heat. Stir in the oatmeal, salt, and baking powder. Mix well.

Pat into greased 8 x 8 x 2 inch baking pan. Sprinkle remaining ingredients on top. Press them into the batter with fingers. Bake in preheated 350°F. oven for 20 to 25 minutes. Cool on cake rack. Cut into thin bars to make about 24.

Mary's Shortbreads

If you like perfect shortbread and if you have an electric mixer make this recipe. The secret of their perfection is lots and lots of beating.

  1 cup butter (no margarine)
  ½ cup icing sugar
1½ cups all-purpose flour

Make sure butter is at room temperature. Place all the ingredients in a mixing bowl. Then beat 10 minutes at medium speed. Scrape bowl twice during beating period. Mixture should have a whipped butter consistency and appearance. Drop by spoonfuls on ungreased cookie sheet (shortbreads will not spread).

Eggplant Tomato Casserole — eggplant, onions, tomatoes, cheese — a five-star luncheon casserole. Recipe on page 50.

Decorate tops with bits of red or green cherries or small pieces of almond, pecan, or walnut.

Bake about 20 minutes in a preheated 300°F. oven or until they show a slight browning around the edges. Cool on cake rack. They will keep for 8 to 10 weeks, packaged in a metal or plastic box with a sheet of waxed paper between each row.

Coconut Marshmallows

Have fun making your own mallow cookies. Place 1 tablespoon of the mallow mixture on top of a cookie before it is set; press a second one on top, sandwich fashion. Use any of your favorite cookie recipes.

- 1 envelope unflavored gelatine
- ⅓ cup cold water
- ½ cup sugar
- ⅔ cup corn syrup
- 1 tsp. vanilla
- ¾ cup finely grated coconut, toasted

Sprinkle gelatine over cold water in saucepan. Place over low heat and stir until dissolved, about 3 minutes. Add sugar and stir until dissolved. Remove from heat. Place corn syrup and vanilla in large bowl of electric mixer. Add gelatine and sugar mixture and beat at highest speed until mixture becomes thick and of soft marshmallow consistency, about 15 minutes. While mixture is beating, grease 2 loaf pans, 7¼ x 3¼ x 3 inches. Use toasted coconut to line sides and bottom of pans thoroughly. Pour 2 cups of the marshmallow mixture into each pan.

Smooth off top with spoon or knife and sprinkle top with more coconut. Let stand in a cool place (not a refrigerator) until well set, about 1 hour. To remove from pan, loosen around edges with a knife, and invert on cookie sheet or board. Cut into squares with a sharp knife moistened with cold water. Roll marshmallows in coconut to coat the sides of the marshmallows.

Tea Dainties

Here are some quick ideas for unexpected guests at tea time:

Hovis bread or any good brown bread well buttered and sprinkled with one's favorite fresh herbs.

Small slices of French bread, buttered and covered with a thin slice of Swiss or cheddar cheese. Sprinkle with basil or tarragon. Brown under broiler. Serve hot or cold.

White bread buttered with cream cheese or cottage cheese, topped with honey, served on a bed of mint. Guests eat mint with bread or sprinkle mint on honey.

Bread or hot biscuits buttered with foie gras sprinkled with tarragon.

Canadian Fritter Batter

In this country we make fritters with fruits, vegetables, and even meat, so our type of batter is somewhat more solid than the French and baking powder is used.

- 2 cups all-purpose flour
- 1 tbsp. baking powder
- 1½ tsp. salt
- 2 tbsp. sugar
- 4 egg yolks
- ⅔ cup milk
- 2 tbsp. melted margarine
- 4 egg whites, stiffly beaten

Sift together the first four ingredients. Beat egg yolks and add milk, then stir into dry ingredients. Stir in the melted margarine; gently fold in the beaten egg whites.

At this point, add 1 to 2 cups of chopped, cooked meat or diced fruit or lightly cooked or blanched vegetables. If you wish a sweeter fruit fritter, add 3 tbsp. of sugar to batter.

Drop large spoonfuls into deep hot fat. Fry 4 to 5 minutes, or until crisp and brown. Serves 6.

Hard Meringue — everybody's favorite, it can be filled with whipped cream, ice cream, fruit, or combinations of all three. Recipe on page 81.

Desserts

Almond Paste Cake

A superb pound cake, easy to make, it surely needs no frosting — delectable thinly sliced, to serve with tea. It freezes very well.

- ¾ cup margarine or half margarine, half butter
- ½ cup diced almond paste
- ½ tsp. almond extract
- 1 tsp. vanilla
- 1 cup fine, granulated sugar
- 3 eggs
- 2¼ cups all-purpose flour
- 1 tsp. salt
- 1 tsp. baking powder
- ¾ cup milk

Butter a 9-inch tube pan or a loaf pan.

Cream the fat with the almond paste, almond extract, and vanilla at medium speed in an electric mixer.

Then add sugar, 1 tablespoon at a time, beating for 30 seconds after each addition, then beat the whole 2 minutes. Add the eggs, one at a time, beating well after each addition.

Sift together the flour, salt, and baking powder. Add to mixture all at once with the milk. Beat by hand until well mixed.

Pour into prepared pan. Bake in a 300°F. oven for about 1¼ hours or until golden in color. Let stand 10 minutes before unmolding. Then turn out on wire rack to cool.

Delicious Cake

Marie Nightingale wrote a most interesting book entitled *Out of Old Nova Scotia Kitchens*, published by Pagurian Press. Out of that book comes this cake, not only delicious, but so versatile, and with great keeping quality. Try it.

Mix, in the following order:

- 1 cup butter (creamed well)
- 2 cups sugar (added gradually)
- ½ cup milk and ½ cup hot water (mixed together

Add to butter mixture, then add the following, beating constantly:

- 1 egg
- 1 cup all-purpose flour
- 1 egg
- 1 cup all-purpose flour
- 1 egg
- 1 cup flour sifted with 1½ teaspoons baking powder
- 2 teaspoons almond extract

When smooth and creamy, pour into a greased 9-inch tube pan. Bake in preheated 350°F. oven for 1 hour or until done.

Let stand 10 minutes, unmold on cake rack to cool.

Sour Cream Chocolate Cake

A self-frosted, one-layer cake that is both attractive and easy to put together.

- 6 tbsp. soft butter or margarine
- 1 cup sugar
- 2 eggs, at room temperature
- 1⅓ cups all-purpose flour
- 1½ tsp. baking powder
- 1 tsp. each, soda and cinnamon
- 1 cup commercial sour cream
- 6-oz. package semi-sweet chocolate chips
- 1 tbsp. sugar

Place the butter, sugar, and eggs in the bowl of an electric mixer and beat at medium speed for 10 minutes. Sift dry ingredients together and blend by hand into creamed mixture. Mix sour cream in well.

Pour batter into a greased and flour-dusted 9 x 13-inch baking pan. Scatter the chocolate chips evenly over top, then sprinkle with a tablespoon of sugar.

Bake in a 350°F. oven for 35 minutes, or until cake just begins to pull away from sides of pan. Cool in the pan on a cake rack and keep at room temperature. To serve, cut into small rectangles or squares.

Glazed Carrot Nut Cake

This cake will keep for three months in the freezer and is useful to have on hand. If you do not want to make the orange glaze, simply put whipped cream on the cake when you are ready to serve.

   1¼ cups salad oil
    2 cups fine granulated sugar
    2 cups all-purpose flour
    2 tsp. baking powder
    1 tsp. each soda and salt
    2 tsp. cinnamon
    4 eggs
    3 cups grated raw carrots
    1 cup finely chopped walnuts or pecans
      glaze (see below)

Beat the oil and sugar with an electric mixer at medium speed for 5 minutes. Sift the next four dry ingredients together and stir half into sugar mixture. Blend thoroughly. Add remaining half of dry ingredients alternately with eggs, one at a time, mixing well after each addition. Add carrots and nuts, mix well, and pour into a lightly oiled 10-inch tube pan. Bake in a 325°F. oven for 1¼ hours. Remove from oven, invert on a cake rack, unmold, and cool.

The glaze: Place in a saucepan 1 cup of sugar, grated peel of ½ an orange, ¼ cup of cornstarch, and 1 cup of fresh orange juice. Stir until well mixed, then add 1 tsp. lemon juice, 2 tbsp. butter, and ½ tsp. salt. Cook over medium low heat, stirring until thick and glossy, about 3 to 5 minutes. Cool until tepid, then spread on unmolded cake. When cool, freeze cake on a tray, then remove cake, wrap, label, and put back in freezer.

First Raspberries Coffee Cake

When the first raspberries ripen in the garden, we eat a large plateful topped with maple sugar and yogurt, to taste. The next day comes the coffee cake, light, tender, perfect with tea. When the raspberries are finished, repeat both treats with blackberries.

   ¼ cup soft butter
   ⅓ cup sugar
    1 tsp. vanilla
   ¼ tsp. grated lemon peel
    1 egg, beaten
    1 cup all-purpose flour
  1½ tsp. baking powder
   ½ tsp. salt
   ⅓ cup milk
    1 cup ripe raspberries

Cream together until fluffy, the butter, sugar, vanilla, and lemon peel. Beat in the egg.

Sift together the flour, baking powder, and salt. Add to creamed mixture alternately with milk.

Spread evenly into a well-buttered 8-inch round cake pan. Sprinkle the raspberries on top.

Mix together 2 tablespoons each of butter and brown sugar, ¼ cup flour, ¼ teaspoon ground cardamon or coriander, until crumbly.

Sprinkle over the raspberries. Bake in a preheated 375°F. oven, 25 to 30 minutes or until cake is done. Cut into wedges and serve warm or tepid, with or without cream.

Coffee Charlotte Russe

In Victorian days, no dinner was complete without Charlotte Russe. As a variation, use the flavoring of your choice (vanilla, rum, brandy, rosewater) to replace the modern touch of instant coffee.

   ½ cup sugar
    1 envelope unflavored gelatin
   ⅛ tsp. salt
    2 tbsp. instant coffee
  1¼ cups milk
    2 eggs, separated
   ½ tsp. vanilla
    1 cup whipping cream
   8 to 12 ladyfingers

Mix together ¼ cup of the sugar, gelatin, salt, and instant coffee in the top of a double boiler.

Beat the milk with the egg yolks and add to the gelatin mixture. Cook over boiling water, stirring constantly, for 5 minutes or until the gelatin has dissolved. Remove from heat, add the vanilla, and refrigerate until the mixture is half set.

Beat the egg whites, add the remaining ¼ cup of sugar, and beat until peaks form. Fold the half-set coffee mixture into the stiff egg whites. Whip the cream and add to the coffee mixture.

Set the ladyfingers in individual molds or in a crystal bowl; pour in the cream and refrigerate for 4 to 12 hours. Serves 8.

Superb Plum Pudding

Another gift from the British settlers.

    ½ cup grated unpeeled apples
    ¼ lb. chopped beef suet
    ¼ cup chopped walnuts
    2 tbsp. diced candied orange peel
    2 tbsp. diced candied lemon peel
    ⅔ cup diced candied citron peel
    1½ cups seedless raisins
    1 cup currants
    1 tbsp. cinnamon
    1½ tsp. ginger
    ¼ tsp. nutmeg
    ½ tsp. allspice
    ¼ tsp. salt
    1 cup sugar
    ⅓ cup apricot jam
    2 cups fine dry bread crumbs
    4 eggs
    2 tbsp. milk
    ⅓ cup brandy or rum
    ⅓ cup white wine or orange juice

In a large bowl, combine all the ingredients except the last four and mix thoroughly. Beat the eggs, then add to them the remaining ingredients. Add to the fruit mixture and mix thoroughly with your hands — a spoon cannot blend this thick mass properly.

Oil and sugar a 1-quart mold or two 1-pint molds. Fill ⅔ full, cover tightly, and steam — the quart for 5½ hours, the pints for 4. Serve with Special Hard Sauce.

Special Hard Sauce

    ½ cup unsalted butter
    1½ cups sifted icing sugar (measure after sifting)
    1 egg yolk
    2 tbsp. rum or brandy

Cream the butter until very light. Gradually add the sifted icing sugar. When it is very smooth, add the egg yolk and the rum or brandy. Beat well, pour into a dish and refrigerate overnight.

Apple Mincemeat

Make ahead of time for Christmas — refrigerated, it will keep 4 months; frozen, it will keep 1 year.

    2 apples
    1 lb. currants
    1 lb. seedless raisins
    ¾ lb. fresh, ground beef suet
    1 lb. brown sugar
    ¾ lb. mixed peel
    3 tbsp. cinnamon
    2 tbsp. allspice
    1 tbsp. ground coriander
    1½ cups dry sherry
    4 tbsp. brandy

Peel, core, and chop apples finely. Place in a bowl with the remaining ingredients and stir for 5 minutes. Pour into hot sterilized jars. Seal when cold. Yield: 3 pints.

Caramel Bread Pudding

I consider this my best bread pudding.

    ¾ cup brown sugar
    2 slices heavily buttered bread
    1 egg, beaten
    1½ cups milk
    1 tsp. vanilla

Pack sugar in a buttered casserole, cut bread in small pieces, and place, buttered side down, on sugar. Mix egg, milk, and vanilla and pour over mixture. Put in oven and bake (350°F.) until nicely browned. Serve with or without cream. Serves 4.

Cream of Liqueur

A smart, delectable, miniature dessert with a sophisticated topping of slivered, toasted almonds, it gleams in small oriental dessert dishes and should be accompanied by a bottle of the same liqueur chosen to make it, a liqueur glass with each dessert, not to sip but to use as a measure to pour over the dessert.

    1¼ cups light cream
    1½ envelopes of unflavored gelatine
    3 egg yolks
    ½ cup sugar
        a pinch of salt
    ⅓ cup liqueur of your choice*
    3 egg whites
    ⅓ cup slivered almonds

Measure the cream in a saucepan. Add the gelatine; let stand 5 minutes. Then stir over low heat until gelatine is melted. Beat the egg yolks with the sugar and salt. Add to the hot cream, stir together 5 or 6 minutes. Remove from heat, stir in the liqueur.

Beat the egg whites until stiff and fold into the gelatine mixture. When well mixed, pour into individual dishes. Refrigerate at least 4 hours or overnight.

Place the slivered almonds on a baking sheet and set in a 325°F. oven until toasted, about 20 minutes. Cool, set aside. Sprinkle to taste over each dish of cream when ready to serve. Serves 8.

*Benedictine, B and B, Cointreau, Kalua Coffee Liqueur, Crème de Menthe, rum, brandy or bourbon are all equally good. Each one gives the dessert a different flavor.

Caramelized Floating Island

A light, creamy, crunchy Victorian delight, this is one of those recipes that varies with every family. One variation is to replace the first half cup of sugar with maple sugar or syrup.

    4 eggs, separated
    1¼ cups sugar
    2½ cups milk
        vanilla or nutmeg, to taste

Beat the egg yolks with half a cup of the sugar until fluffy. Beat egg whites until soft peaks appear. Add ¼ cup of sugar and beat again until stiff.

Heat milk to a simmer in a large saucepan, then drop in egg white by heaping tablespoonfuls. When well puffed turn quickly to cook other side. As soon as done, remove with a skimmer to a hot platter. These egg white balls take but a minute to cook.

Add yolks to milk and stir quickly until you have a lovely golden cream (do not allow it to boil). Flavor to taste and pour over egg whites.

Over medium heat, caramelize remaining sugar with 3 tbsp. of water to obtain a light golden syrup. Using a fork, pour caramel in long shreds over egg snow. Refrigerate until cold. Serves 6.

Orange and Lemon Snow

Snows are used mostly for desserts. Basically they are a sweet, light, fluffy aspic — very nice as a garnish for fruit salads. Vary the fruit juice; frozen undiluted concentrate can be used. It usually comes in 6-oz. cans, so water, apple juice, or fresh orange juice can replace the balance of the liquid.

    1 envelope unflavored gelatine
    ½ cup sugar
    ¼ tsp. salt
    1½ cups fresh orange juice
    ¼ cup fresh lemon juice
    2 unbeaten egg whites
        peel of 1 orange and 1 lemon, grated

Mix the gelatine thoroughly with the sugar and salt in a small saucepan. Add ½ cup of the orange juice. Heat over low heat, stirring constantly until the gelatine has dissolved.

Remove from heat and stir in the remaining orange and lemon juice. Chill until slightly thicker than an unbeaten egg white.

When ready, add the unbeaten egg whites and the grated peel of orange and lemon, and beat with an electric beater until mixture foams and begins to hold its shape. Spoon into a glass dessert dish or into small molds. Chill until firm.

To serve as a dessert, top with thawed frozen berries of your choice, or a custard sauce made with the remaining 2 egg yolks. Serves 8.

Golden Snow Fluff

Cool and light, this dessert is superb served with fresh strawberries, sweetened with Cointreau, Grand Marnier, or sugar. The sauce is served separately.

    2 envelopes unflavored gelatine
    ½ cup cold water
    ½ cup boiling water
    1 cup sugar
    ½ tsp. salt
    1 cup fresh grapefruit juice
    1 cup fresh orange juice
    4 eggs, separated
    2 cups light cream or milk
    ⅓ cup sugar
      pinch salt
      grated peel of 1 orange

Soak the gelatine in ½ cup of cold water for 5 minutes. Add boiling water and stir until gelatine has dissolved. Add sugar, salt; stir again to dissolve sugar (over low heat, if necessary). Add the two juices, mix, and refrigerate until the consistency is that of unbeaten egg whites. Then beat with a rotary beater until fluffy.

Beat egg whites until stiff and fold into fruit fluff. Pour into a glass dish, cover, and refrigerate until set.

Orange Custard Sauce: Beat egg yolks with cream or milk, sugar, and salt. Cook in top of double boiler over medium-high heat to a light custard consistency, stirring often. Add orange peel, pour into a jug and refrigerate. Serves 10.

Macaroon Rice Pudding

This scrumptious rice pudding with its almond macaroon crusted top is equally delicious hot or cold. Serve as is or with table cream or whipped cream.

    4 cups milk
    ½ cup sugar
    ⅓ cup uncooked, short grain rice
      pinch salt
    2 tbsp. soft butter
      enough almond macaroons to cover top
    1 egg, beaten
    ½ tsp. vanilla
    ½ tsp. almond essence

Place in buttered 1½-quart casserole the milk, sugar, rice, salt, and butter.

Bake uncovered, in 325°F. oven for 1½ hours, stirring 4 to 5 times during cooking period.

Remove from oven, cover top with macaroons, rounded side up. Beat egg with vanilla and almond essence, pour over macaroons, and bake another half hour. Serves 6.

Lemon Rice Cream

Creamy, tasty, easy to make, this rice cream will keep for 4 to 6 days, well covered, in refrigerator.

    1 cup uncooked, short grain rice
    4 cups milk
      pinch salt
    3 pieces lemon rind
    4 tbsp. sugar
      cinnamon or nutmeg

Put all ingredients except the cinnamon or nutmeg in a heavy metal saucepan.

Cook, uncovered, over low heat, for 1 hour. Stir a few times during the cooking period.

Pour into serving dish. Sprinkle with cinnamon or nutmeg. Cover and refrigerate until cold. Serve as is or with raspberry jam or thawed frozen strawberries.

Jam Omelette

This is one of the easiest dessert omelettes. I make it at the table in an electric frying pan — everybody enjoys the proceedings, which seem to double the pleasure of eating the result.

    1 tbsp. butter
    1 tbsp. blanched almonds, slivered
    6 eggs
    1 tbsp. sugar
    3 tbsp. cold water
    1 tbsp. red currant jelly
    2 tbsp. raspberry jam or jelly

Melt the butter in the omelette pan and brown the slivered almonds. Beat the eggs lightly with the sugar and cold water. Pour over the almonds and cook according to directions. When ready, place the red currant jelly and raspberry jam or jelly in the middle, and fold the omelette. Serves 4 to 5.

Treacle Tart

This Norfolk specialty is true to the original recipe when made with golden syrup and English black treacle. My version has no bread crumbs, and it freezes very well.

    pie dough of your choice
    1 cup golden syrup
    2 tbsp. treacle
    2 tbsp. butter
    grated rind of ½ a lemon
    2 eggs, well beaten with
    3 tbsp. cream

Line an 8-inch pie plate with pie dough, bake, and cool. Warm syrup, then add treacle. Remove from heat, add butter, lemon rind, and stir until butter has melted. Add the eggs, beaten with cream and stir thoroughly.

Pour into cooled crust and cook in a 350°F. oven until custard is set, about 15 to 20 minutes. Cool, then top with whipped cream or chopped walnuts. Serves 4 to 6.

Note: The golden syrup and treacle can be replaced by 1¼ cups of molasses for a slightly different flavor.

Maple Tourlouche

This is a sort of quick upside-down cake and a must during the sugaring season in eastern Canada. It should be served hot with cold rich cream poured on top. As a variation, add some chopped walnuts to the hot syrup.

    1 cup maple syrup
    1 tbsp. soft butter
    3 tbsp. sugar
    1 egg
    1 cup all-purpose flour
    2 tsp. baking powder
    ⅛ tsp. salt
    ¼ tsp. nutmeg or cinnamon
    ½ cup milk

Bring syrup to a boil and pour into a generously buttered 8 x 8 x 2 inch baking dish. Let stand in a warm place. With a large spoon or blending fork, beat butter, sugar, and egg together until creamy.

Mix remaining dry ingredients and add with the milk to creamed mixture, stirring until well blended. Place as four large balls into hot syrup, then stretch dough with two forks until all are joined together. This is easy because the dough gets very soft when it comes in contact with the hot syrup.

Bake at 350°F. for 30 minutes, or until golden brown. When done, invert onto a platter or serve directly from pan.

Sugar Pie

Every summer, requests pour in for this sugary, yet creamy pie from people who have travelled in Quebec and have had it in restaurants. The recipe is almost as old as Canada.

    pastry of your choice
    ½ tsp. soda
    ¼ tsp. vanilla
    1½ cups maple syrup
    1 cup all-purpose flour
    1 cup dark brown sugar
    pinch nutmeg
    ⅓ cup butter

Line a 9-inch pie plate with pastry. Stir soda and vanilla into syrup and pour into pastry. Blend remaining ingredients with your fingertips until mixture is crumbly, then spread over syrup. Place a piece of foil under pan, because the pie often bubbles over. Bake at 350°F. for 30 minutes and let cool — it is best cold.

Lemon Cream Chiffon Pie

A moist, lemony delight.

    1 cup whipping cream
    1¼ cups sugar
    2 tbsp. cornstarch
    1 envelope unflavored gelatine
    ¼ tsp. salt
    1 cup water
    3 eggs, separated
    ½ cup fresh lemon juice
    2 tbsp. butter
    1 tsp. freshly grated lemon peel
    1 baked 9-inch pastry shell

Allow ⅓ cup of cream to stand at room temperature for 10 minutes. In saucepan, combine 1 cup sugar, cornstarch, gelatine, and salt; blend in water until smooth. Beat yolks until light. Blend into cornstarch mixture along with lemon juice and butter. Bring to a boil over medium heat, stirring constantly; boil 2 to 3 minutes. Remove from heat. Stir vigorously while gradually adding 1/3 cup cream and lemon peel. Transfer to metal bowl. Chill mixture in ice water until it mounds slightly when dropped from a spoon. It should be cool but not cold. Meanwhile, beat egg whites to soft peak stage. Gradually add remaining 1/4 cup sugar, beating until whites are stiff, but still glossy and moist. Whip remaining 2/3 cup of cream until stiff. Gently fold egg whites and cream into chilled mixture. Spoon into baked pastry shell. Chill until firm.

The Best of Lemon Pies

Through the years, I have made many lemon pies, as they are my favorites. None is better or creamier than this one, with a perfect meringue.

  1½ cups sugar
  ¼ cup plus 2 tbsp. cornstarch
  ¼ tsp. salt
  ½ cup cold water
  ½ cup fresh lemon juice
  3 egg yolks, well beaten
  2 tbsp. butter or margarine
  1½ cups boiling water
  1 tsp. freshly grated lemon peel
    few drops yellow food coloring
  1 baked 9-inch or 2 8-inch pastry shells

In a 2 to 3-quart saucepan, mix together sugar, cornstarch, and salt, using a wire whisk. Still using whisk, gradually blend in cold water, then lemon juice until smooth. Add beaten egg yolks, blending very thoroughly. Add butter or margarine. Add boiling water gradually, stirring constantly with rubber spatula. Gradually bring mixture to full boil, stirring gently and constantly with spatula over medium to high heat. Reduce heat slightly as mixture begins to thicken. Boil slowly for 1 minute. Remove from heat and stir in grated peel and food coloring. Pour hot filling into baked pastry shell. Let stand, allowing a thin film to form while preparing meringue.

Meringue
  3 egg whites
  ¼ tsp. cream of tartar
  6 tbsp. sugar

Have egg whites at room temperature. Using a small, deep bowl beat egg whites with electric mixer several seconds until frothy (some fairly large air cells still remain). Add cream of tartar. Beat at high speed until whites have just lost their foamy appearance and bend over slightly when beaters are withdrawn, forming soft peaks. Reduce speed to medium while gradually adding sugar, about a tablespoon at a time. Return to high speed and beat until whites are fairly stiff but still glossy and soft peaks again form when beaters are withdrawn. Place meringue on the hot filling in several mounds around edge of pie. Using a narrow spatula, push meringue gently against inner edge of pie crust, sealing well. Cover the rest of the filling by spreading meringue from edge of pie to centre, forming decorative swirls with spatula. Bake at 350°F. for 12 to 15 minutes until golden brown. Cool on wire rack at room temperature away from drafts for 2 hours before cutting and serving. Use sharp knife and dip into hot water after each cut for a perfect clean-cut serving. Yield: 1 large deep 9-inch pie or 2 8-inch pies.

Hard Meringue

This recipe can be made into small individual meringues or a large shell that can be filled with a cream mixture, ice cream, fruits, etc. It will keep, ungarnished, for three weeks in a covered metal or plastic container in a cool, dry place.

  2 egg whites
    pinch of salt
  ¼ tsp. cream of tartar
  ½ cup superfine sugar
  ¼ tsp. extract of your choice

Beat egg whites with salt and cream of tartar to a soft foam. Sprinkle 1 tsp. of the sugar over the surface and beat until completely incorporated. Continue adding sugar, 1 tbsp. at a time, until all the sugar is added. Beat in the flavoring and continue to beat until the mass holds its shape.

Sprinkle a baking sheet with flour or cover it with freezer paper or parchment (found in department stores at kitchen and freezer counters).

To shape small to medium-size meringues, use a spoon or a pastry bag and drop the meringues on to the prepared baking sheet, leaving ½ inch between them.

To make a shell, shape meringue into a round 8 to 10 inches in diameter directly on baking sheet, or in a 8, 9, or 10-inch pie plate; gently flatten the middle with the back of a spoon.

Bake in a 300°F. oven until the meringues reach a delicate pale brown, 20 to 60 minutes depending upon size and shape.

Red Wine Jelly

A cool, colorful dessert to be made a day or so ahead and served as is, or surrounded with sweetened berries, or topped with strawberry ice cream.

> 2 tbsp. unflavored gelatin
> ¼ cup cold water
> 2 slices lemon peel
> 1 cup boiling water
> ½ cup sugar
> 1 cup gooseberry jelly
> 1 cup dry red wine
> 2 tbsp. brandy or lemon juice

Soak the gelatine in the cold water 5 minutes. In a saucepan, simmer lemon peel, boiling water, sugar, and jelly over low heat until sugar and jelly are dissolved.

Add gelatine, stir to dissolve, then put mixture through a sieve. Add remaining ingredients, pour into individual molds or a 1-quart mold and refrigerate until set. Serves 6.

Granita di Caffe

This refreshing Florentine specialty is one of the most simple frozen desserts to prepare, but nothing can beat the pleasant refreshing sensation of Granita on a hot afternoon. Black roasted coffee is used in the original recipe, but I have found that instant coffee gives a deeper flavor.

> 4 tbsp. instant coffee
> 2 cups boiling water
> ¼ to ½ cup sugar
> 2 tsp. vanilla or 1 tsp. aromatic orange bitters
>   (Angostura)
> whipped cream (optional)

Combine the instant coffee, boiling water, and ¼ to ½ cup sugar (according to taste) in a sauce-pan and stir over medium heat just until the sugar has dissolved. Do not boil the mixture. Cool and add the vanilla or bitters. Pour mixture into a shallow pan or a refrigerator freezing tray and freeze until almost firm. Turn into a bowl and beat well — an electric hand beater is ideal because it will beat more air into the mixture and make it lighter. Freeze until it is the consistency of sherbet.

To serve, spoon into sherbet glasses or punch cups and top with unsweetened, whipped cream. Serves 4.

The Ice Cream Bar

All these sauces can be prepared ahead of time and kept refrigerated in serving containers. Set them out with a bucket of ice cream, plates, spoons, and let everybody go to town.

Melba Sauce: Bring to a boil ½ cup of red or black currant jelly, 1 tbsp. of cold water, ⅛ tsp. of salt, ½ cup of raspberry jam, and 1 tbsp. of lemon juice. Remove from heat and cool before refrigerating. Yield: 1 cup.

Fluffy Tropical Topping: Combine 6 oz. of undiluted frozen orange juice with 1 cup of cream, whipped. Fold in ½ cup of moist, shredded coconut, and 1 tsp. of grated orange rind. Yield: 2 cups.

Butterscotch Cream Sauce: Place in a saucepan ¾ cup of sugar, 1⅓ cups of brown sugar, ¾ cup of corn syrup, ¼ cup of butter, and ½ cup of undiluted evaporated milk. Stir constantly over medium heat until sugar has dissolved and sauce is well blended. Add another ½ cup of evaporated milk and stir 1 minute. Cool, then add ½ tsp. of vanilla. Yield: 2 to 2¼ cups.

Toffee Sauce: This one should be served hot. Place contents of a 1-lb. bag of caramels in the top of a double boiler over water kept hot, but not boiling. Cover and let melt, then stir in ½ cup of hot water. Yield: 2 cups.

Hot Fudge Sauce: Place in a saucepan 3 squares (1 oz. each) of unsweetened chocolate, 1 cup of sugar, 1 cup of corn syrup, ½ cup of light cream or evaporated milk, and 2 tbsp. butter. Cook over medium heat, stirring constantly, until mixture comes to a full rolling boil. Boil briskly for 3 minutes, remove from heat, and add 1 tsp. of vanilla.

If made ahead of time, refrigerate and reheat by placing in a pan of hot, not boiling, water until sauce has thinned to pouring consistency. Yield: 2 cups.

Coffee Ice Cream: The easiest of all. Simply have your guests sprinkle instant coffee granules to taste over their vanilla ice cream. It is even more scrumptious topped with a chocolate sauce.

If you do not like the idea of a self-serve table, try one of these combinations:

Six ounces of undiluted frozen orange juice over a brick of chocolate ice cream.

Drained and mashed canned peaches plus grated orange rind over strawberry or vanilla ice cream.

Continental Ice Cream

This is a great dessert to serve when raspberries are in season. Although it is easy to make, it is quite elegant.

1 pint fresh raspberries
¼ to ½ cup red currant jelly
2 tbsp. brandy or port (optional)
6 dry almond macaroons
¼ cup slivered almonds
1 pint raspberry or strawberry ice cream

Clean the raspberries. Melt the currant jelly over low heat and pour over the berries. Stir gently with a rubber spatula until all the berries are covered with the jelly. Add the brandy or port and refrigerate until ready to serve.

Crumble the macaroons coarsely and mix in the almonds. To serve, put the ice cream in sherbet glasses and top with a generous portion of the raspberry sauce. Sprinkle with the macaroon-almond mixture. Serves 6.

Fruit

When the fresh fruit season is at its height, satisfy your sweet tooth with these recipes. Or, simply top the fruit with a cooked grain such as buckwheat.

Slice unpeeled oranges, then toss with pitted black olives and sweet onion rings. Serve on crisp lettuce, topped with lemon-orange dressing (see below).

Thinly slice peeled and cored pears, add chopped chives or green onions, seedless grapes, a pinch of fennel seeds, and serve on lettuce with French dressing.

Finely chop 8 to 10 fresh mint leaves, stir with 1 tbsp. of honey and refrigerate for at least an hour. One hour before serving, section 4 grapefruits into a glass dish, top with honey-mint and refrigerate again. Stir before serving.

Frost grapes to eat with lightly buttered whole-grain bread (dark rye, crushed wheat). Spread clear honey on a cluster of grapes, using a pastry brush, then dip in finely ground dry coconut. Small bunches of different colored grapes are very attractive.

For a delectable uncooked fruit mousse, beat 3 egg whites with ¼ cup of honey until stiff. Without cleaning beaters, beat 3 yolks with another ¼ cup of honey until fluffy. Fold two mixtures together and add 2 to 4 cups of diced fruits. Top with grated orange rind, finely chopped nuts, and refrigerate. Serves 4.

For Cherries à la Parisienne, fill a glass bowl with fresh cherries (they do not have to be pitted), top with a few spoonfuls of honey, and let stand 4 hours at room temperature. Stir and serve topped with sour cream or yogurt.

To make lemon-orange dressing for fruit salads, mix ⅓ cup of fresh orange juice and safflower or peanut oil, ¼ cup of fresh lemon juice, 1 tbsp. of honey, 1 tsp. each of curry powder and salt. Keep refrigerated and shake well before using. Yield: 1¼ cups.

For a fruit salad French dressing that does not have to be refrigerated, mix ¼ cup of fresh lemon or lime juice, 1 tbsp. of sweet vermouth, ¾ cup of peanut oil, 1 tsp. of salt, 1 tsp. of crushed dried mint, and, if you wish, ¼ tsp. of crushed dried tarragon. Shake well before using. Yield: 1½ cups. (You can substitute cider vinegar for the vermouth, but then you have to refrigerate the dressing, and this one, like most dressings, is very much better served at room temperature.)

Breakfast Fruit

The following are just a few suggestions for a sparkling start to a Sunday breakfast. I leave my fruit at room temperature overnight to bring out the full flavor.

Fresh strawberries, sweetened to taste and marinated in fresh orange juice, look lovely served in crystal cups, as do peeled oranges, in slices or sections, topped with chopped pecans or walnuts and a dash of sherry.

Angostura bitters can be used for more than cocktails. Halve a grapefruit, remove seeds, loosen sections, sprinkle each half with 1 heaping tsp. of maple or brown sugar and about 10 drops of bitters. Cover and let stand overnight, or, you can wait and prepare it 10 minutes before serving.

Apples and oranges are also a good overnight-stand combination. For 6 people, peel 4 oranges and slice thinly. Peel and core 3 apples and slice thinly. Place fruit in alternate layers in a glass dish, sprinkling each layer with sugar (I use a total of ½ a cup in all, you may want more). Sprinkle with the juice of ½ a lime or lemon, cover, and let stand.

If you want something exotic and spectacular, serve hot brandied citrus. For 4 people, carefully peel and section 1 large grapefruit and 2 oranges the night before. Arrange layers alternately in a shallow buttered dish and squeeze the juice of 2 oranges on top. Mix 3 tbsp. of brown sugar with ½ tsp. of mace or nutmeg and sprinkle over. Dot the whole thing with 2 tbsp. of butter, then pour 2 to 4 tbsp. of brandy on top. When ready to serve, bake for 25 minutes at 325°F. This can also be served cold — omit the butter, cover, and leave overnight at room temperature. The sugar will melt and form a syrup.

Then, there are always moons of canteloupe, with the juice of half a lime squeezed on top of each. Sweeten with fruit sugar.

And, finally, a delicious combination is to thaw the contents of 1 package of frozen strawberries, pass them through a sieve or blender, and use as a syrup over fresh raspberries.

Fruit Compotes

Strawberry Compote

Wash and hull 1 quart of strawberries. Place in a bowl and dribble ¼ to ½ cup of honey over them. Add the grated peel and juice of half an orange. Stir gently with your fingertips, cover, and refrigerate.

Raspberry Chantilly Compote

Thaw a 10-oz. package of frozen raspberries, then mash with a fork or in a blender. Put through a sieve to remove seeds. Clean 1 quart of fresh raspberries. Whip 1½ cups of whipping cream, flavor with 2 tbsp. of icing sugar, and 3 tbsp. of brandy or 2 tsp. of vanilla.

Pile the cream in the centre of a glass dish, surround with fresh raspberries, and spread raspberry purée gently over berries. Serve with a basket of hot biscuits; each guest pouring the compote over the biscuits.

Black Cherry Burgundy Compote

Stem and pit 1 lb. of large B.C. Bing cherries and place in a pan with ¼ cup of honey and ¼ cup of red Burgundy or port. Cook over low heat until red juice oozes out of the cherries. Stir in 2 tbsp. of cornstarch, and the juice of half an orange or 3 tbsp. of rum. Keep stirring until mixture is creamy and transparent. Serve hot or cold with hot biscuits.

Superb Peach Berry Compote

Peel and slice enough fresh peaches to fill an 8-oz. measuring cup. Pour them into a serving dish and do the same with an equal quantity of hulled fresh strawberries or blueberries. Mash contents of two 1-pint baskets of raspberries with 3 tbsp. of icing sugar and pour over fruit in bowl. Sprinkle generously with icing sugar, cover, and refrigerate. The mixture is stirred only when you are ready to pour it over the biscuits. Yield: 3 to 4 cups.

Blueberry or Fresh Currant Compote

Stem, wash, and dry 4 cups of blueberries or currants and place in a serving dish. Combine ¼ cup of corn syrup, 1 tbsp. of grated orange peel,

¼ cup of fresh orange juice, and bring to a boil. Simmer over low heat for 3 minutes, then stir in 3 tbsp. of honey and pour over fruit. Cover and let stand at room temperature. When cool, refrigerate. If you wish, add 3 tbsp. of orange liqueur or brandy before serving. Yield 3 to 4 cups.

Hot Bread Apple Charlotte

This Charlotte is a family version of the rich, crusty, French classic. It must be served hot, with lots of sweetened whipped cream flavored with a few drops of almond extract.

Dough base:
  1 cup flour
  ½ tsp. baking powder
  ¼ tsp. salt
  2 tbsp. sugar
  3 tbsp. soft butter
  2 eggs, beaten
  2 to 3 tbsp. milk

Filling:
  5 cups sliced peeled apples
  ½ cup seedless raisins
  1 cup apple juice
  ¼ cup rum
  ⅔ cup sugar
  1 tsp. cinnamon
  grated rind of ½ lemon

To make the dough, sift together the flour, baking powder, salt, and sugar. Cut in the butter and work in smoothly with a wooden spoon. Beat in the eggs. Stir in the milk. The dough must be stiff yet somewhat soft, so be careful with the milk.

Grease an 8-inch springform pan. With a rubber spatula or spoon, spread dough on the bottom and part way up the sides of the pan. The top edge will look ragged.

The filling: Place in a saucepan the apple slices, raisins, and apple juice. Cook, uncovered, over medium heat until the apples are soft, but have not lost their shape. Strain over a bowl. Place liquid back in the saucepan, add the rum, and boil until syrupy. Set aside.

Combine the sugar, cinnamon, and lemon rind. Stir gently into the apple-raisin mixture. Spoon into the dough-lined pan. Bake in preheated 425°F. oven 50 to 60 minutes or until crust is a deep golden brown and filling is firm. Cool 10 minutes. Open spring mold and slide Charlotte onto plate. Warm rum syrup and pour all over dough and apples. Serves 6.

Caramel Apple Crumble

An unusual apple-crisp type dessert.

  4 large apples
  1 cup light brown sugar
  ½ tsp. cinnamon
  2 tbsp. rum
  1 cup all-purpose flour
  ½ tsp. salt
  1 cup grated medium cheddar cheese
  ½ cup soft butter

Peel, core, and slice the apples thinly into an 8-inch baking dish. Mix ½ cup of the brown sugar with the cinnamon and rum. Sprinkle on the apples and mix lightly.

Combine flour, salt, grated cheese, butter, and remaining ½ cup brown sugar.

Crumble mixture evenly over the apples. Bake in a 325°F. oven, 40 to 45 minutes. Serve warm with sour cream or whipped cream. Serves 4.

Shaker Boiled Apples

The simplicity of this dessert accounts for its delicate flavor. Serve quite cold.

  6 red cooking apples, unpeeled and uncored
  cold water or apple juice
  ½ cup sugar

Place apples in a large saucepan. Add half an inch of water to the saucepan. Pour sugar over apples. Boil gently about 20 minutes or until apples are tender. Turn apples carefully several times. Serve with the sugar syrup. Serves 6.

Croquants aux Pommes

An old recipe from Quebec. Almost like a bonbon. Serve as is or with ice cream.

Peel, core, and slice 2 large apples. Place in a bowl with ½ cup chopped nuts. Beat 1 egg with 1 cup sugar until well beaten to partly dissolve the sugar. Add 2 tablespoons flour and 1 teaspoon baking powder and ⅛ teaspoon salt. Pour into a 9-inch pie plate. Bake 35 minutes in a 375°F. oven, or until top is browned. Chill 6 to 8 hours before serving. Serves 4.

Apple Pancakes

A luncheon dessert or a breakfast treat. Serve with a bowl of cinnamon sugar: a teaspoon of cinnamon mixed with a cup of sugar.

> 2 eggs, beaten
> 1⅞ cups milk
> 2 cups flour
> 4 tbsp. baking powder
> 2 tbsp. sugar
> 1 tsp. salt
> 2 tbsp. melted butter
> 4 medium apples, peeled, cored, and grated
>   juice and grated rind of 1 lemon

Add beaten eggs to milk, whip a few seconds. Sift together the flour, baking powder, sugar, and salt. Add to milk mixture; stir only enough to moisten dry ingredients. Stir in the melted butter — again do not beat as texture toughens if beaten. Combine the grated apples, lemon juice, and rind. Add to pancake batter.

Bake on greased hot griddle or frying pan over medium high heat, turning only once when bubbles appear on top. Serve. Yield: 15 to 20 medium pancakes.

Poached Peaches

These peaches keep 6 to 8 days if refrigerated. Poaching them with the skin on makes all the difference in the flavor.

> 2 cups water
> 1 cup sugar
> 1 vanilla bean or 4 to 6 inches orange peel or
>   3 to 4-inch cinnamon stick
> 6 to 12 unpeeled peaches

Bring to boil in a deep stainless steel frying pan, the water and sugar with the vanilla bean or orange peel or cinnamon stick. When boiling, place the unpeeled peaches in the syrup, one next to the other. Cover and poach for 20 minutes over low heat. Transfer peaches to a dish. Boil syrup, uncovered, until it is thick. Remove peels and stones of peaches (very easy) and pour thickened syrup on top. Cover and serve cold. Serves 6 to 8.

Tangerine Compote

This compote will freeze well for up to 5 months at 0°F. Thaw it for 4 to 6 hours before you serve it.

> 2 navel oranges
> 6 tangerines
> ½ cup honey
> 1 cup fresh orange juice
>   grated peel of 1 orange
> 3 tbsp. orange liqueur (optional)

Peel the oranges and slice them paper thin. Peel tangerines and break into sections. Put them in a bowl in alternating layers, sprinkling each with a dribble of honey.

Boil orange juice with peel 15 minutes over medium-low heat. Let cool, add liqueur, and pour over fruit. Cover and refrigerate. Serves 4 to 6.

Portuguese Sweet

The Portuguese refer to this easy sweet as "rapido." It is that, and very pleasant as well.

> 6 to 8 tangerines
> 8 tbsp. bitter marmalade
> 3 tbsp. rum or tangerine juice
>   grated unsweetened chocolate

Peel tangerines, break into sections, and place in a dish. Boil marmalade and rum or juice over medium heat for 2 minutes, pour over fruit sections, cover, and refrigerate. Serve topped with as much grated chocolate as you like. Serves 4 to 5.

Fresh Strawberry Pie Glacé

Glacé is the French way of flavoring fresh fruit pie without cooking the berries. It is beautiful to look at and very fragrant.

> 4 cups fresh strawberries
> 1 cup sugar
> 1 tbsp. cornstarch
> 1 tsp. grated lemon peel
> 1 tbsp. lemon juice
>   10-inch pie shell, baked

Crush 1½ cups of the strawberries with a fork, add the sugar, cornstarch, lemon peel, and juice. Stir together until well blended. Cook over medium heat until transparent, stirring most of the time.

Fill the baked shell with the rest of the strawberries, placing them point up. Pour over the hot berry syrup, which should completely cover the berries with a shiny topping — the *glacé*. Chill and serve. Serves 6 to 8.

Strawberry Rhubarb Cobbler

What an affinity there is between strawberries and rhubarb! This superb pudding would not be nearly as good made with just the strawberries or rhubarb alone.

1½ cups sugar
1 cup apple juice
½ cup water
2 cups diced rhubarb
2 cups sliced strawberries
1 tsp. vanilla
1 cup all-purpose flour
2 tbsp. sugar
1½ tsp. baking powder
½ tsp. mace
¼ cup butter
¼ cup milk or cream
  sugar and nutmeg
  soft butter

Bring the sugar, apple juice, and water to a boil and stir until sugar has dissolved. Remove from heat, add the rhubarb, strawberries, and vanilla. Mix well and pour into a pudding dish.

To prepare the batter, sift together the flour, sugar, baking powder, and mace. Cut in the butter and add the milk or cream. Stir quickly to blend, and drop by spoonfuls over the fruit. Sprinkle top with sugar and a dash of nutmeg, and brush with soft butter. Bake at 450°F. for 20 to 25 minutes. Serves 6.

Strawberries Nevers

I have a friend who sends me a jar of superb homemade Seville orange marmalade every year, which I keep to make this dessert. The preparation is simplicity itself — the result is luscious.

1 qt. fresh strawberries
1 cup Seville orange marmalade
¼ cup orange-flavored liqueur or brandy
½ cup fresh orange juice
1 tsp. grated orange rind
1 tsp. lemon juice
  whipped cream (optional)

Wash strawberries before hulling them. Drain thoroughly on an absorbent towel. Hull.

Mix marmalade with liqueur or brandy over low heat and stir until well blended. Add orange juice gradually, while stirring, until enough is used to give a medium-thick sauce. Add orange rind and lemon juice.

Put the strawberries in a cut-glass dish and pour the cooled marmalade sauce over them. Refrigerate for at least 2 hours before serving.

Serve with a bowl of whipped cream, sweetened with a little marmalade and flavored with orange-flavored liqueur or brandy. It is good without the cream too. Serves 6 to 8.

Strawberry Rhubarb Compote

I need many superlatives to describe this early summer delight. Serve it in a glass dish with a bowl of whipped, sour, or ice cream.

½ cup orange juice
¾ cup sugar
2 lbs. rhubarb, cut into 2-inch pieces
1 pint fresh strawberries, or, 10-oz. pkg. frozen strawberries

Bring the orange juice and sugar to a boil; stir until sugar has dissolved. Add rhubarb, simmer over low heat for 5 minutes, and remove from heat.

Stir in fresh (cleaned and halved) or frozen strawberries (the hot mixture will thaw them); refrigerate. Serves 4.

Variations with Fresh Strawberries

Try these delicious tricks with fresh strawberries:

Cover with brown sugar or grated maple sugar — top with sour cream.

Sweeten with strawberry jam diluted with hot apple or orange juice.

Mix equal quantities of strawberries and cubes of fresh pineapple, sweeten to taste, and pour fresh orange juice on top.

Pour orange juice mixed with finely chopped fresh mint over the berries. Sprinkle the whole with icing sugar. Chill thoroughly and serve heaped in fruit cocktail glasses.

Whip 1 cup cream, fold it into 1 pint of soft strawberry ice cream. Serve over the sweetened berries.

For delicious, unusual muffins, replace the 1 cup of milk in your favorite muffin recipe with 1 cup crushed sweetened strawberries. Add 1 extra tbsp. butter or shortening.

Whip 1 cup cream, sweetened with ½ cup clear honey and 2 tbsp. crushed strawberries. Serve with a bowl of berries.

Six Desserts for Impatient Gourmets

Cake and Ice Cream

Mix a devil's food or chocolate cake according to directions on the package. Then beat in 2 tsp. instant coffee, 1 tsp. cinnamon, ¼ tsp. cloves, and 1 tsp. vanilla. Bake in layers. To serve, put slightly softened ice cream (vanilla or chocolate) between the layers.

Broiled Cake

Bake a white cake in a single layer. Remove it from the oven, and, while warm, spread it with a mixture made up of 3 tbsp. melted butter, 6 tbsp. brown sugar, 2 tbsp. cream, 2 tbsp. sherry, ½ cup shredded coconut, and ¼ cup chopped walnuts. Put the cake under the broiler a minute or two until golden brown.

Fresh Strawberry Delight

Crush a pint of strawberries lightly — do not mash. Stir for a few minutes with 1 cup sugar and 1 tsp. lemon juice. Pour the strawberries over a cooled angel food cake. Serve with a dish of whipped cream sweetened and flavored with vanilla.

Banana Cake Dessert

Mix a yellow cake mix as directed on the box. Just before pouring the batter into the pan, add 1 cup mashed ripe banana pulp and the grated rind of 1 orange. Bake as directed. Serve with whipped cream and shredded coconut.

Cherry Jubilee Parfait Pie

Add ⅓ cup brandy to the drained contents of a can of pitted dark sweet cherries. Let stand overnight. Save the cherry juice, and the next day heat and add enough boiling water to make 1 cup. In this dissolve 1 package of raspberry gelatine. Add the brandy drained from the cherries. Then stir in by spoonfulls 1 pint of vanilla ice cream — stirring each time until melted. Chill the mixture until slightly thickened. Then fold in the drained cherries. Turn into a baked and cooled 9-inch pie shell. Chill, but do not freeze it too hard.

Eggnog Parfait Pie

Dissolve a package of lemon gelatine in a cup of hot water with 2 tbsp. sugar. Stir in by spoonfuls a pint of vanilla ice cream — stirring until melted. Add 1 tsp. vanilla and 1 tsp. rum flavoring. Chill until half set, then blend in 2 eggs that have been beaten until foamy. Turn into pie shell. Sprinkle with nutmeg and chill. Ice cream pies are best when smooth and not hard frozen.

Classic of Haute Cuisine

Drain canned pitted Bing cherries, peaches, and pineapple chunks. Mix the juices. Add juice of 1 lemon to 1 cup of mixed fruits. For the *haute cuisine* touch, add brandy to taste, but be lavish with it. Serve cold.

French Chef Special: Start with a bought readymade chiffon cake. Roll cake in 1 cup maple syrup beaten with ¼ cup rum. (Yes, a bit sticky.) Then roll cake in finely shredded coconut, or finely chopped nuts. Top with rum-flavored whipped cream.

Shortcake in Five Minutes: Place a bought, readymade, double-layer sponge cake in a 350°F. oven for 5 minutes, just to heat. Squeeze juice of 2 oranges (no law against adding a little rum to it). Slowly pour orange juice over hot cake. Pour 1 box thawed-out frozen berries on top. No cream is needed. Delicious just exactly as is.

A Summer Cheese Soufflé, Golden Eggs Mayonnaise, fresh strawberries, and bread sticks — a lovely combination of tastes, textures, and colors. Recipes on pages 47 and 61.

Jams and Jellies

13

Winter Strawberry Jam

A few boxes of frozen strawberries with a generous touch of dry port wine — in a few minutes you have a superb jam all year around.

   3 packages (10 oz.) frozen sliced strawberries
   1 package (1¾ oz.) powdered pectin
   6 cups sugar
   4 pieces lemon rind
   1 cup dry port
   3 tbsp. fresh lemon juice

Thaw the strawberries. Combine with pectin in a large saucepan and bring to a fast rolling boil, stirring often. Boil for 1 minute. Add the sugar and the pieces of lemon rind; bring again to a rolling boil and boil hard for 1 minute.

Remove from heat, stir in wine and lemon juice. Let stand for 5 minutes, stirring occasionally. Remove the lemon rind. Pour into hot sterilized glasses. Seal at once with melted paraffin. Yield: 6 to 7 (8-oz.) glasses.

Apple Jam My Way

I like apple jam, not apple jelly. I am very fond of fresh green ginger and enjoy a light touch of wine, so I invented this recipe which I have used for many years.

   5 cups finely diced unpeeled apples
   3 tbsp. grated fresh ginger
   1¼ cups water
   1 package (1¾ oz.) powdered pectin
   5 cups sugar
   ½ cup red or rosé wine or dry apple cider or red Spanish wine*
   ¼ cup fresh lemon juice

English Muffins, homemade jam, and tea — a winning combination. Recipe on page 105.

Combine apple, ginger, water, and pectin in a large saucepan. Bring to boil and boil for 2 minutes. Stir in the sugar, bring to a full rolling boil, and boil hard for 1 minute more. Remove from heat and add the wine or cider of your choice, and the lemon juice. Let stand for 5 minutes, stirring 3 or 4 times. Skim off the foam. Pour into hot sterilized jars and seal at once. Yield: 6 (8-oz.) glasses.

*Each wine will give a different flavor and color.

Cucumber Jelly

A clear, green jelly, excellent with ham or duck, or, for afternoon tea with cream cheese and toasted muffins.

   2 lbs. whole cucumbers
   3 tbsp. water
   1 lb. sugar (or 2 cups)
     juice of 1 lemon
   1 tsp. grated fresh ginger root or 1 tsp. ground ginger

Wash cucumbers, cut into slices, and place in saucepan with the water. Bring to boil over medium heat. Crush down with a large spoon or blending fork. Cover and simmer for 30 minutes, stirring a few times. Strain through a jelly bag.

For each pint of juice, use 1 lb. of sugar. Place sugar in saucepan, bring to a fast rolling boil, stirring all the time. Add the lemon juice and ginger, then boil over medium heat until it passes the jelly test. Pour, while hot, into small jam jars. Cover and turn upside down to cool. (If a jar leaks, it means the cover is badly adjusted or not tight). Keep in cool place.

Tomato Lemon Jam

An old-fashioned preserve that never loses its appeal. My grandmother used either red or yellow tomatoes to make this recipe.

5 lbs. firm tomatoes, peeled
5 lbs. sugar
3 unpeeled lemons, thinly sliced
1 tbsp. grated fresh ginger root or 1 tsp. ground ginger

Coarsely chop peeled tomatoes and place in a saucepan in alternate layers with sugar and lemon slices. Add ginger (fresh, if possible) and, stirring frequently, simmer slowly over medium-low heat until thick, about 45 to 50 minutes (it must become the consistency of jam). Pour into hot sterilized glasses and seal immediately. Yield: 4 to 5 glasses, 6 oz. each.

Peach Rum Jam

Use to top chocolate cake, instead of icing. Serve as dessert with toasted English muffins and thinly sliced Swiss cheese.

4 cups prepared, ripe peaches (about 3 lbs. or 2 qts.)
5 cups (2¼ lbs.) sugar
1 box powdered fruit pectin
¼ cup dark rum

First, prepare the fruit. Peel and pit about 3 pounds of fully ripe peaches. Grind or chop very fine. Measure 4 cups into a very large saucepan.

Now make the jam. Measure sugar and set aside. Add powdered fruit pectin and rum to fruit in saucepan and mix well. Place over high heat and stir until mixture comes to a hard boil. Add sugar all at once. Bring to a full rolling boil and boil hard for 1 minute, stirring constantly. Remove from heat and skim off foam with metal spoon. Then stir and skim by turns for 5 minutes to cool slightly, to prevent floating fruit. Ladle quickly into glasses. Cover jam at once with ⅛-inch hot paraffin. Yield: about 9 medium glasses (4½ lbs. jam).

Mary Milroy's Beet Jelly

Serve with ham, use to glaze roast of pork for a rosy hue, or just enjoy it with toasted home-made bread.

2 cups cooked beets
7 cups sugar
1½ cups cider or Japanese vinegar
1 bottle liquid pectin (Certo)

Grate beets on fine grater or pass through meat chopper. Measure the 2 cups as full as possible.

Place the sugar and vinegar in a large saucepan. Add the beets. Mix thoroughly and bring to a fast rolling boil, stirring a few times. Remove from heat and stir in the pectin, then keep stirring for 5 to 8 minutes, almost constantly. This stirring prevents the beets from floating and cools the jam slightly. Pour in jam jars and seal.

Cranberry Tangerine Relish Cups

A festive turkey should be accompanied by a festive garnish. This relish will do any bird proud.

8 tangerines
8-oz. can whole cranberry sauce or 2 cups fresh sauce
⅛ tsp. mint extract

Cut about one-fourth off the stem end of each tangerine. Using a large spoon and working over a bowl, insert the tip of a spoon between the tangerine's meat and outer peel. Revolve the tangerine, working the spoon farther in each time and pulling the meat away — as it becomes loosened it is easy to insert the spoon all the way and gently scoop out the entire centre in one piece, leaving a perfect tangerine shell.

Do the same with each tangerine, setting the shells aside. Working over the same bowl, separate tangerine centres into sections, removing any seeds. Mix with juice, remaining ingredients, and chill. Spoon into shells and serve with turkey, chicken, duck, goose, pork, or ham. Serves 8.

Beverages

14

Dutch Milk Punch

Make this punch in a blender in front of your guests and serve it in chilled punch cups or wine glasses filled with crushed ice.

1 cup brandy
2 cups cold milk
4 tbsp. fine sugar
½ tsp. vanilla
fresh nutmeg, to taste

Pour the brandy into blender with milk, sugar, and vanilla. Cover and blend at high speed until mixture is frothy. Pour over ice and grate a dash of nutmeg on top. Serves 6.

California Cold Duck

I was surprised when I saw "Cold Duck" on a menu in California and was ready to pass it by. Now I'm glad I didn't; it is a perfect before-dinner drink on a summer night.

6 cubes sugar
2 cups fresh orange juice
26-oz. bottle extra-dry domestic champagne, chilled

Use 6 champagne glasses, 5 or 6-oz. capacity. Place 1 cube of sugar in each: divide fresh orange juice equally among glasses; top with well-chilled champagne. Serves 6.

Kir

Abbé Kir of France is credited with the creation of this simple but sophisticated drink.

⅓ cup Crème de Cassis* or Cherry Heering liqueur
26 oz. bottle Chablis or other good dry white wine, chilled

Chill six 6-oz. wine glasses. Pour 1 tbsp. of the Crème de Cassis into each, top with chilled wine, and stir. Serves 6.

*Use the black currant liqueur or non-alcoholic syrup.

My Zippy Fresh Blender Cocktail

A blender is absolutely necessary for this recipe — an interesting way to use celery leaves.

2 well-packed cups celery leaves
2 thinly sliced unpeeled lemons
4 to 6 tbsp. honey or maple syrup

Place all the ingredients in the blender jar and almost fill it with water. Cover and blend for 3 minutes at high speed. Pass the mixture through a coarse strainer, then add more water to taste. Serve very cold or over ice.

The straining is not absolutely necessary — the small specks of lemon and celery leaves are pleasant to munch. Serves 7 to 9.

Raspberry Punch

In the summer I use fresh berries — two large cupfuls crushed with the sugar and strained to remove the seeds.

1 box frozen raspberries
¼ cup sugar
    grated rind of 1 orange
¼ to ½ cup brandy
1 bottle red wine
    (Canadian Bordeaux-type or imported rosé)
1 bottle sparkling red wine or 1 large bottle
    soda

Place the frozen raspberries in a bowl, add the sugar to taste, and grated orange rind. Let stand until the berries have thawed and the sugar has melted. Add brandy. (If desired, the mixture may be strained to get rid of the raspberry seeds.) Mix well and add the red wine. This mixture may be kept in bottles, refrigerated, for 3 to 5 weeks.

To serve — pour mixture into a bowl and add the sparkling wine or soda. Serves 8.

Romanian Pickup

Prepare this recipe the night before for a healthy, invigorating start to a busy day.

1 sweet apple
    juice of ½ a lemon
10-oz. carton plain yogurt
    clear honey, to taste

Wash and core apple, then slice it thinly or grate on a medium grater. Mix immediately with the lemon juice. Add yogurt, stir, and dribble honey on top. Cover and refrigerate overnight. Serves 1.

Five-Star Spring Dinner

The arrival of spring calls for a celebration, and a good way of celebrating it is with a great dinner. This one serves 8; most of it can be prepared in advance.

Cream of Curry Soup
Golden Cheese Crisps
Chicken Pie Terrapin
Green Peas Robert
Divine Strawberry Torte

Cream of Curry Soup

Serve this with the Cheese Crisps, or with garnishes of chopped green onion, grated unpeeled apple tossed with lemon juice, crumbled crisp bacon, and chopped hard-boiled eggs. Pass a tray with a small bowl of each garnish and let your guests choose their favorite.

1 onion, finely chopped
2 tsp. curry powder
⅓ cup butter
⅔ cup flour
3 cups chicken bouillon
3 cups light cream
   salt and pepper, to taste
¼ cup dry sherry (optional)

Simmer onion with curry powder and butter, stirring most of time, until onion is soft but not browned. Add flour, mix thoroughly, then add bouillon and cream. Stir or, preferably, beat with a wire whisk until soup starts to boil. Simmer over low heat for 15 minutes.

If making the day before, let soup cool; refrigerate. Reheat when needed.

Add salt, pepper, and sherry.

Golden Cheese Crisps

They can be served either with drinks or with the soup. Prepare them in the morning, set on a baking sheet, and heat when needed.

1 cup grated strong cheddar cheese
½ cup mayonnaise
¼ tsp. Worcestershire sauce
1 tsp. prepared mustard
½ tsp. turmeric
   sesame seeds or finely chopped walnuts
   crackers, any type

Blend cheese with mayonnaise, Worcestershire sauce, mustard, and turmeric. Spread on crackers and sprinkle with seeds or nuts. Bake at 400°F. for 5 to 8 minutes and serve warm. Yield: about 24.

Chicken Pie Terrapin

This chicken, with its special sauce and garnish of forcemeat balls, may seem like a lot of work, but the result is a beautiful and tasty pie that your guests will long remember.

2 chickens, 3 lbs. each
¼ cup flour
1 tsp. salt
½ tsp. pepper
½ tsp. tarragon or ¼ tsp. thyme
3 tbsp. butter
3 tbsp. salad oil

Cut chicken into serving pieces. Roll pieces in mixture of flour and seasonings until well coated. Heat butter and oil in a large frying pan and brown 5 or 6 chicken pieces at a time until golden. When all are browned, put back into frying pan, cover, and simmer over low heat for 30 minutes.

In the meantime, make a stock with necks, gizzards, and bits of skin removed from chicken. Now prepare forcemeat bread balls as follows:

**8 slices crustless white bread
grated peel of 1 lemon
1/3 cup chopped parsley
1/4 tsp. thyme
1/8 tsp. nutmeg
1 tsp. salt
1/4 tsp. pepper
1/3 cup soft butter
2 egg yolks**

Chop bread very fine, or if it is stale, grate on a coarse grater. Mix thoroughly in a bowl with lemon peel, parsley, and seasonings. Add butter and egg yolks, and work into a smooth paste. Form into 1-inch balls by rolling with hands on a board. Set on a platter and refrigerate.

Then make savory forcemeat balls:

**livers and hearts of 2 chickens
1 1/2 cups twice-ground cooked ham
1/4 cup chopped parsley
4 green onions, finely chopped
salt and pepper, to taste**

Pass livers and hearts through a meat grinder and add to remaining ingredients. Blend, then form into 1-inch balls as for bread balls. Brown both sets lightly in butter.

**pastry of your choice
2 tbsp. cornstarch
1/2 cup cream, any type
1 beaten egg yolk or milk**

To assemble pie, line a large casserole with pastry, put chicken in and place forcemeat balls among the chicken pieces. To juices remaining in frying pan, add 1 cup of strained chicken stock and boil fast, scraping bottom.

Mix cornstarch into cream, add to pan, and stir over medium heat until creamy. Pour sauce over contents of casserole. Brush edge of crust with egg yolk or milk. Top casserole with pastry, pinch edges together, and cut one slit in centre. Bake at 350°F. for 50 to 60 minutes, or until a deep golden color.

Green Peas Robert

A French chef, Robert, who is a master at cooking vegetables, uses frozen peas in this excellent recipe.

**4 slices of bacon, diced
1 small onion, chopped
2 tbsp. butter
2 pkgs. frozen green peas, 10 oz. each
1/4 cup shredded lettuce leaves
1/2 tsp. sugar
salt and pepper, to taste**

Fry bacon until crisp and drain on absorbent paper. Brown onion in bacon fat, remove, then drain fat from pan. Put butter in same pan, and, when melted, add frozen peas, lettuce, and sugar.

Cover tightly and simmer until peas have separated. Stir to mix, break up any stuck together, then cover again and cook until tender. Add bacon and onion, stir until hot, season, and serve.

Divine Strawberry Torte

A wonderful party dessert, this torte cuts easily into wedges. The strawberries may be replaced with raspberries, peaches, or blueberries, depending on the season. Everything can be done ahead of time.

**1/2 cup egg whites
1 tbsp. lemon juice
pinch of salt
1 1/3 cups fine granulated sugar
1/2 cup flaked coconut
2 egg yolks
pinch of salt
2 tbsp. lemon juice
2 tbsp. sugar
1 tbsp. cornstarch
1/2 cup water
1 cup whipping cream
1 to 2 pints fresh strawberries**

Using hand mixer or electric beater, beat egg whites with lemon juice and salt until soft peaks are formed. Add sugar, 3 tbsp. at a time, beating hard after each addition. Keep beating until a stiff meringue is formed, 10 to 15 minutes in all. Gently fold in coconut.

Mark a 9-inch circle on a baking sheet and grease inside lightly. Turn meringue into centre of circle and carefully spread to edges, building up until about 2 inches high around outside and slightly lower in centre. Enclose outer edge with a 2-inch foil collar.

Place in an oven that has been at 400°F. for 15 minutes. Immediately turn heat off and let meringue stand in closed oven for 5 hours. Open door and leave in oven 5 hours more or overnight.

Lemon Sauce: Beat egg yolks with salt, lemon juice, and sugar. Stir in cornstarch and water. Cook in double boiler or over low heat until mixture thickens, beating often. Refrigerate, covered, until cold, then fold in cream, whipped until stiff.

To serve, slip meringue shell on to a serving plate with a large spatula. Top with the lemon cream and arrange sweetened berries on top. Serve at once or refrigerate for 2 hours.

Grand Diner

This elegant dinner can be almost completely prepared the day before. It is one that deserves a beautiful setting — a lace tablecloth, silver, crystal, candlelight, and flowers. Serves 16.

Tapenade de Nice with Crudités
Melon Alcantara
Paupiettes of Sole "à l'Ecossaise"
Vegetables Jardinière
Watercress Salad
Hot Brioches
Peaches Dijonnaise
Filtered Coffee

Wines:

Iced Champagne served with tapenade
Dry Sherry served with melon
Chablis — Premier Cru served with fish
French Liqueur served with coffee

Tapenade de Nice

A *tapenade* is a delicious French dip for vegetables. It can be served at the table with Champagne or more casually with drinks before dinner.

1 crust dry bread
1 clove garlic
3 tbsp. red wine vinegar
¼ lb. pine nuts (pignolia)
3 tbsp. capers
4 fillets of anchovy
2 hard-boiled eggs
12 black olives, pitted
¼ cup parsley, minced
1 cup olive oil
salt and pepper, to taste
1 cucumber
1 green pepper
2 carrots
6 hard-boiled eggs
1 can artichoke hearts

Remove crust from a slice of bread, cut peeled garlic in two, rub both sides of the bread with the garlic. Break up the bread in a bowl, pour the vinegar on top. Work bread and vinegar with the fingers until it is mushy.

At this point, the work can be done either in a blender or by passing the ingredients through a food chopper. Place in the blender the bread, nuts, capers, fillets of anchovy, the yolks of the two hard-boiled eggs (save whites for salad), black olives, parsley, and the split clove of garlic. Add half a cup of the olive oil. Blend until creamy. Gradually add the rest of the olive oil. When well blended, add salt and pepper to taste. The process is the same with the food mill, adding the oil gradually as the food is chopped.

Pour the mixture into a glass dish that can be fitted into an elegant bowl filled with ice. The tapenade can be prepared two or three days ahead of time, but keep it refrigerated.

To serve, make small sticks of the cucumber, green pepper, and carrots; cut the 6 hard-boiled eggs into quarters. Drain the artichoke hearts and spread on absorbent paper until thoroughly dry.

Place the prepared vegetables and eggs on ice around the dish of tapenade sauce. Serve with a glass of cold Champagne.

Melon Alcantara

Prepare individual servings in small ovenware dishes; refrigerate overnight, if desired. To serve, place in oven as indicated in the recipe.

2 canteloupes
1 Spanish melon
4 limes
salt
1 tbsp. fresh grated ginger
freshly grated nutmeg
¼ lb. butter

Make balls of canteloupe and melon, making a mixture of five to seven for each dish, depending on the size of the dish. Salt and pepper and grate a dash of nutmeg over each dish. Cut the butter into small dice and divide evenly over each dish. Mix the freshly grated ginger and lime juice, divide evenly on top of the melon, cover, and refrigerate. When ready to serve, place for 20 minutes in a 350°F. oven.

Paupiettes of Sole "à l'Ecossaise"

This dish can be prepared in the morning, and reheated before dinner.

2 lbs. fresh salmon
2 eggs
½ cup minced parsley
1 tsp. tarragon, fresh or dried
1 tsp. salt
½ tsp. pepper
18 fillets of sole
grated rind of 3 lemons
1 bottle dry white wine
¼ cup butter
½ cup flour
1 cup rich cream
½ cup milk
3 tbsp. brandy
salt and pepper, to taste
½ tsp. sugar
1 tbsp. butter
1 lb. fresh thinly sliced mushrooms, or, 1 large box of imported chanterelles
½ tsp. monosodium glutamate
1 green onion, chopped fine
salt and pepper

Pass the uncooked salmon, which has been filleted, through a food chopper twice. Add the eggs, parsley, tarragon, salt, and pepper, and beat with a whip or a wooden spoon until creamy and blended.

Spread sole fillets on a table, salt and pepper each one lightly, and sprinkle with a pinch of lemon rind. Spread the top with some of the salmon mixture, roll, and tie with a thread.

In a large frying pan, warm the white wine but do not let it boil. Place half the rolled fillets in the hot wine and simmer for 10 minutes over low heat, basting constantly with the hot wine. Remove the fillets and place them next to each other on a service platter which can stand oven heat. Cook all the fillets in the same manner. Carefully remove the thread from each fillet.

Pass the cooking wine through a fine strainer and set aside. In the same frying pan, melt the ¼ cup butter, add flour, stir until very well blended, pour the strained wine over, add the cream and milk. Stir constantly with a wire whip, over medium heat, until you have a smooth, velvety sauce. Then add the brandy, sugar, salt, and pepper to taste. Stir again for a few minutes. Taste for seasoning. If sauce is too thick, add a little milk or cream gradually, while stirring, until the consistency is right. Set aside.

Melt 1 tablespoon of butter. When light brown, add the mushrooms, monosodium glutamate, chopped green onion. Stir half a minute over high heat. Place here and there around the fish. Now divide the sauce equally over each fillet of fish, leaving some of the mushrooms uncovered.

When ready to serve, place in a preheated 400°F. oven for 15 to 20 minutes.

Vegetables Jardinière

Make a selection of small green beans, small carrots, and round balls of potatoes or any other mixture of vegetables that you like. Blanch, butter, mix, and serve. Use 4 lbs. of vegetables for 16 people.

Watercress Salad

Combine watercress and Bibb lettuce in a salad bowl. Toss with a plain French dressing and garnish with the finely shredded remaining two egg whites from the tapenade.

Peaches Dijonnaise

The flavor combination of peaches, praline, custard, and coffee and brandy syrup has to be savored slowly to be fully appreciated. Fantastic!

8 peaches
1 cup fresh orange juice
grated rind of two oranges
½ cup black currant syrup
1 cup sugar
1 cup water

Wash the peaches but do not peel. In a large frying pan with a cover, place the orange juice and rind, the black currant syrup, sugar, and water. Bring to a fast rolling boil, while stirring. Place the unpeeled peaches in the syrup; cover, lower the heat, and simmer 25 minutes turning once. Remove from heat, uncover.

While the peaches are cooking, prepare the praline mixture.

Praline

2 cups sugar
juice of ½ a lemon
1 cup bleached almonds
1 cup unbleached hazelnuts

In a saucepan combine the sugar and lemon juice, stir constantly over medium heat until it has turned into a light golden syrup, add the nuts, stir until well mixed, and pour mixture into a jelly roll pan, spreading the nuts and the syrup as evenly and as quickly as possible. Set aside until cold, which will take about one hour. Then, either crush in a blender at high speed, a bit at a time, removing the blended part before adding more, or, butter a rolling pin and crush a few pieces at a time over a wooden board. Set aside.

Peel the cooled peaches; cut in half. Place a half, rounded side up, in individual custard cups or in a soufflé dish; sprinkle 2 tablespoons of the praline over each and top with the following cream mixture.

French Cream

5 whole eggs
4 egg yolks
1 cup sugar
4 cups light cream
1 cup milk
1 vanilla bean

Beat together lightly the whole eggs, egg yolks, and sugar. In the meantime, warm up the cream and milk with the vanilla bean. When hot, remove the vanilla bean, beat into egg and sugar mixture. Divide equally over the praline and peach.

Place the individual dishes in a pan of hot water, bake in a 350°F. oven until the blade of a knife comes out clean. When ready and cooled, refrigerate overnight or until ready to serve.

Serve with Dijon Syrup made in the following manner.

Dijon Syrup

1 cup sugar
1½ cups water
4 tbsp. vanilla
4 tbsp. coffee liqueur
1 tbsp. brandy

Place the sugar in a frying pan, stir over medium heat until it turns into a light golden syrup. Remove from heat. Add the cold water, a tablespoon at a time. When all is added, put back over the heat and cook, stirring occasionally, until the mixture becomes a light syrup. Remove from heat and cool. Then add the vanilla, coffee liqueur, and brandy. Mix well. Place in a jar and refrigerate until ready to be poured over each dessert. This sauce will keep, refrigerated, for 2 to 3 weeks.

Beef Fillet Dinner

A simple but elegant dinner for 6.

Milli Fanti Consommé
Beef Fillet Connaught
Swedish Glazed Potatoes
Poblano Beets
Ruby Applesauce

Milli Fanti Consommé

¾ cup fresh fine bread crumbs
½ cup grated Parmesan cheese
2 whole eggs, beaten
salt and pepper, to taste
⅛ tsp. grated nutmeg
6 cups hot chicken or beef consommé

Blend together the bread crumbs, Parmesan cheese, and eggs. Add salt, pepper, and nutmeg. Pour into the hot consommé. Cover and simmer over low heat for 8 minutes. Beat with a whisk and serve.

Beef Fillet Connaught

1 3 to 3½-lb. beef fillet
3 tbsp. butter
1 tbsp. salad oil
3 to 4 onions, thinly sliced
1 tsp. strong prepared mustard
1 tbsp. chutney
¼ cup Madeira wine

Trim and tie the fillet. Heat the butter and oil in a large frying pan. Brown fillet on both sides, over high heat, turning all the time. Set aside in dripping pan. Add onions to remaining fat in the pan. Brown over medium heat.

Meanwhile, blend the mustard and chutney. Salt and pepper the fillet. Spread chutney mixture on top and pile onions over it. Pour Madeira around.

Roast in preheated 400°F. oven for exactly 30 minutes, for rare, 40 for medium to well done. Make gravy with canned beef consommé, undiluted, added to pan drippings.

Swedish Glazed Potatoes

Boil 6 to 8 unpeeled, medium-sized potatoes. Do not overcook. Drain. Cool. Peel and set aside, covered. This can be done 6 to 8 hours before dinner. Keep covered at room temperature. When meat gravy is ready, pour ¼ cup in frying pan, add 1 teaspoon butter and ½ teaspoon thyme. Add potatoes, stir, uncovered, over medium heat, until golden and hot. Serves 6.

Poblano Beets

4 beets
¼ cup grapefruit or orange juice
½ tsp. sugar
1 tbsp. butter
1 tbsp. lemon juice
1 cup seedless grapes

Peel and grate the raw beets; combine with the grapefruit and orange juice, sugar, butter, and lemon juice. Cover and simmer for 1 hour, stirring occasionally. Twenty minutes before the end of the cooking period, add the grapes. The fruit juice may be replaced by grape juice or red wine.

Ruby Applesauce

4 to 5 cups blue Concord grapes
6 apples
½ to 1 cup sugar
1 lemon
whipped cream (optional)
grated unsweetened chocolate

Wash the grapes. Pinch the skins from the pulp; reserve the skins.

Put the pulp in a saucepan, bring to a boil, and simmer for about 5 minutes. Put through a strainer to remove the seeds.

Peel the apples, core, and slice thinly. Put the apples, grape pulp and skins, sugar to taste, and the juice and grated rind of the lemon in a saucepan. Bring to a boil, while stirring.

Simmer over medium heat for 8 to 12 minutes until the sauce has some texture. Taste for sweetness and add more sugar if necessary, but remember, the sauce will be sweeter when it is cold.

Serve well chilled, with or without whipped cream and grated chocolate.

This sauce can be frozen for 12 months. It takes 3 hours to defrost at room temperature. Serves 8 or more.

Salmon Dinner

A wonderful dinner for 6.

Sea Island Broiled Grapefruit
Victoria Salmon
Molded Fresh Mint Relish
Wild Rice Chasseur
Chinese Broccoli
Swedish Cream

Sea Island Grapefruit

3 grapefruits, cut into halves
¼ cup honey
4 tbsp. rum
½ tsp. ground cardamon
½ tsp. butter, for each half grapefruit

Mix together the honey, rum, ground cardamon. Spread on grapefruits. Top with butter. (If prepared ahead of time, wrap in foil paper.)

To serve, place under broiler, unwrapped, 3 to 4 inches away from heat. Broil 4 to 6 minutes.

Molded Fresh Mint Relish

1½ envelopes unflavored gelatine
2 tbsp. water
1 cup hot water
8 whole cloves
10 aniseeds
¼ tsp. salt
¼ cup sugar
½ cup brandy
½ cup grapefruit juice
¼ cup each fresh lime and lemon juice
¼ cup chutney
¼ cup minced fresh mint

Add the gelatine to the cold water. Let stand 5 minutes.

Place in a saucepan the hot water, cloves, aniseeds, salt, sugar. Boil 5 minutes. Add brandy and grapefruit juices. Stir in the lime and lemon juice and the gelatine. Refrigerate until half set.

Stir in the chutney and minced fresh mint. Oil 6 individual molds. Fill. Refrigerate until set.

Chinese Broccoli

1 lb. broccoli
3 tbsp. salad oil
1 small onion, diced
2 tbsp. soya sauce
1 tsp. sugar
pinch monosodium glutamate
½ cup chicken stock
1 tsp. cornstarch

Wash the broccoli and cut into 1-inch pieces. Heat the salad oil in a heavy frying pan and brown the onion. Then add the broccoli and cook over medium heat, stirring constantly for 3 minutes. Add soya sauce and sugar. Blend together the cornstarch and chicken stock. Add to the broccoli. Keep stirring over high heat for 1 minute.

Victoria Salmon

2 lbs. fresh salmon fillet
salt, pepper, paprika
lemon juice
flour
unsalted butter

Cut salmon fillet on an angle to make slices about ⅜ of an inch thick. Marinate in fresh lemon juice for 20 minutes. Dip in flour which has been seasoned with salt, pepper, and paprika, and fry in melted, unsalted butter for about 20 or 30 seconds on each side. Drain on paper towel. Garnish with parsley and lemon and serve immediately.

Wild Rice Chasseur

¾ to 1 cup wild rice*
2 tbsp. brandy
1 tbsp. curry
3 to 5 tbsp. chutney
¼ cup butter
salt and pepper, to taste

Wash the rice several times in cold water. Boil 4 cups water. Add 1 teaspoon salt and 1 cup rice. Cover and simmer for 20 to 30 minutes. Simmered wild rice does not lose its nutty flavor.

In a cup mix together the brandy and curry. Add the chutney.

Combine chutney mixture and rice, season to taste, add the butter, and stir with a fork until it has melted. Serve.

*You may replace the wild rice with a mixture of "Long Grain and Wild Rice" which is sold in packages.

Swedish Cream

2 envelopes unflavored gelatine
¼ cup cold water
1 pint heavy cream
1 cup sugar
2 cups commercial sour cream
1 tsp. vanilla extract
1 tsp. rosewater (optional)

Sprinkle gelatine over water. Let stand 5 minutes.

Heat heavy cream but do not boil it. Add the gelatine and sugar and stir until completely dissolved. Cool to room temperature.

Fold sour cream, vanilla extract, and rosewater (optional) into the gelatine mixture. Pour into a dish and chill until set.

Serve plain, or, top with sugared fresh fruits, thawed frozen fruits, or jam.

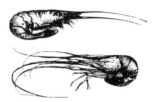

Any Time of the Year Buffet

All recipes serve 6 — double or triple as needed.

Melon Consommé (spring and summer) or
Piquant Pink Bouillon (autumn and winter)
Seafood Superb
Flemish Chicken Casserole
Rice Pilaff Orientale
Carrots Italienne
Braised Onions
Elegant and Casual Baba au Rhum
Café Noir

Melon Consommé
Budget minded: top with minced chives or parsley.

For sheer elegance: top with caviar (Danish lumpfish gives the elegance without the cost). For a summer garden lunch: serve followed by cucumber sandwiches, cheese sticks, and a basket of fruit.

2 cups melon balls
½ cup sherry
3 cans beef consommé
⅓ cup commercial sour cream
    minced chives, parsley, or caviar

Depending on the season, choose the best melon or canteloupe available. Make the balls with a special little spoon called a baller, either small or large. Place in dish that can be covered. Pour sherry on top and refrigerate overnight. Refrig-

erate also for the same period the unopened cans of consommé and the caviar.

To serve, open cans, place a few melon balls in the bottom of the cups, add a teaspoon of the sherry, cover, by teaspoonfuls, with half a can of the chilled, jellied consommé. Top each with teaspoon of sour cream, a dot of minced chives or parsley or caviar on top of the cream. Can be prepared 25 to 40 minutes before serving and kept refrigerated.

Piquant Pink Bouillon
Serve boiling hot, garnished with a half slice of lemon or float a crescent of peeled avocado on top. This delicious bouillon is a combination of ready-to-serve foods.

1 (8-oz.) can tomato sauce
1 (10½-oz.) can beef bouillon
2 can measures of cold water
1½ cups tomato juice
1 tsp. sugar
½ tsp. prepared horseradish
    grated rind of ½ a lemon or 1 lime
⅛ tsp. tarragon or basil or thyme
¼ cup dry red wine

Combine in a saucepan all the ingredients except the wine. Simmer for 15 minutes. Taste for salt and pepper. Add the wine. When hot, serve.

Seafood Superb
A superb buffet salad — prepare all the ingredients a day or two ahead of time. Keep refrigerated in separate containers. An hour before serving, blend together and garnish. Vary the seafood according to the season. Fresh cooked salmon and crabmeat are very springlike. Use large shrimps in the winter, lobster in the fall.

12 to 18 medium-sized shrimps, cooked and
    peeled
1 (7-oz.) can crabmeat
1 hard-cooked egg, coarsely chopped
1 cup celery, finely chopped
4 red radishes, grated (in season)
1 medium carrot, grated
    juice of 2 lemons
½ tsp. salt
⅛ tsp. mace
⅛ tsp. savory
1 to 1½ cups special dressing

Special Dressing

> 1 to 1½ cups mayonnaise
> 1 tbsp. French mustard
> 1 tbsp. catsup
> ½ tsp. chili sauce
> 1 tbsp. each chopped pimiento and green
>   pepper
>   minced chives and parsley, to taste
> 1 hard-boiled egg, chopped fine
> 1 tsp. prepared horseradish

To serve, place the shrimps in a mixing bowl; pick over the crabmeat to make sure all bones are removed, and add to the shrimps, along with the egg, celery, radishes, carrot, and lemon juice. Make the dressing by mixing the ingredients thoroughly, then add enough to the salad mixture to flavor well. Season with the salt, mace, and savory. Blend gently but thoroughly. Set on a platter garnished with lettuce leaves, wedges of tomato, and red radishes. Refrigerate until ready to serve. Can be assembled 1 hour before serving.

Flemish Chicken Casserole

The surprise is beer — the Flemish touch. Cook the day before the party; reheat, covered, in a 300°F. oven when ready to serve. This dish freezes well. Three Cornish hens, split in half, can replace the chicken.

> 3 to 3½-lb. chicken or 3 chicken breasts split
>   in half
> 3 tbsp. butter
> 1 large onion, diced
> 2 stalks celery, finely chopped
> 2 medium carrots, peeled and chopped
> ¼ tsp. marjoram
> ½ tsp. pepper
> 1 tsp. salt
> 1 tbsp. brown sugar
> 3 slices bacon
> 12 ounces light beer
>   juice of ½ a lemon
> 1 tsp. cornstarch
> 1 tbsp. water or brandy

Cut the chicken into small individual pieces or divide each chicken breast in two. Melt the butter in an ovenware casserole (an enamel cast-iron type has the Flemish touch). Add the onion, carrots, celery, and marjoram; stir over low heat until the vegetables are well buttered. Add the salt, pepper, and brown sugar. Stir again to mix and add the chicken. Stir to combine and top the whole with the slices of bacon. Cook, uncovered, in a preheated 400°F. oven for 20 minutes. Then add the beer, cover, and cook another 30 to 45 minutes or until the chicken is tender. At this point, cool and refrigerate, or, freeze.

To serve, heat until bubbly in a 300°F. oven. Blend together the lemon juice, cornstarch, and cold water or brandy. Add to the sauce while stirring until slightly thickened. Taste for seasoning.

Rice Pilaff Orientale

An easy, easy way to cook rice — you can replace the currants or raisins with toasted almonds, lots of minced parsley, grated carrots, chopped green onions, a teaspoon of curry, or turmeric blended with a tablespoon of brandy — each seasoning will give an entirely different flavor to the rice.

> 3 tbsp. margarine
> 1 medium-sized onion, chopped
> 2 cups long grain rice
> 4 cups cold water or chicken bouillon
> 1 tsp. salt
> ¼ cup currants
> ¼ cup boiling apple juice or white wine

Melt the margarine in a saucepan; add the onion. Stir over high heat until onion is buttery; add the rice, and keep stirring until rice has toasted to a light brown color. Lower heat if necessary. Then add, all at once, the 4 cups cold water or chicken bouillon and salt. Boil over high heat, uncovered, until the water covering the rice has been absorbed. This takes about 5 minutes.

In the meantime, pour the boiling apple juice or white wine over the currants. When the rice is ready, add the currants, stir, cover, and cook 20 minutes over very low heat. The rest of the liquid will be absorbed by the rice, which will be beautifully cooked, each grain separate. Uncover; stir with a fork. Cover until ready to use. It will stay hot for 25 minutes.

To make the day before, cook, cool, refrigerate covered. To serve, pour ¼ cup water in saucepan, add the rice, cover, and steam over low heat for 15 minutes, stirring once. It is then hot and ready.

Carrots Italienne

These are equally good served either hot, at room temperature, or tepid. To vary, replace the Marsala wine with an equal quantity of Madeira or port. For luncheon, use as a garnish for broiled liver and bacon. For dinner, serve with roast chicken or veal.

> **1½ lbs. (about 10 or 12) carrots**
> **2 tbsp. butter or margarine**
> **¼ tsp. sugar**
> **½ cup Marsala wine**
> **¼ cup water**
> **minced parsley or chives**
> **salt and pepper, to taste**

Peel and cut the carrots into long matchsticks. Melt the butter. When possible, use a stainless steel saucepan. Add the carrots; stir gently until they are well coated with butter. Sprinkle with sugar. Add the Marsala and water. Bring to a boil. Cover, then simmer over very low heat for 20 minutes. Uncover and boil over high heat until liquid evaporates, but be careful not to let them burn. Salt and pepper to taste. Pour into serving dish. Sprinkle with parsley or chives. Serve hot or cover and let stand until ready to serve.

Braised Onions

For a party I use small white onions, about 1 to 2 inches in diameter — but all sizes are tasty braised in this way. Only the cooking time varies as larger onions are juicier. Cook onions until tender.

> **24 small white onions**
> **½ cup chicken or beef consommé (canned type, undiluted)**
> **2 tbsp. butter**
> **½ tsp. thyme**
> **2 stalks parsley, left whole**
> **½ a bay leaf**
> **salt and pepper, to taste**

Peel the onions. Place in a heavy metal saucepan, just large enough to accommodate all the onions in a single layer. (I use a large frying pan.) Pour the undiluted consommé on top of the onions, add the butter, thyme, parsley, and bay leaf. Bring to a boil, then cover and simmer, about 25 to 30 minutes or until onions are tender. Uncover, boil hard for 5 minutes. Salt and pepper to taste. Pour into serving dish. Serve hot or cooled to room temperature. When served hot, top with paprika; at room temperature, surround with watercress.

Elegant and Casual Baba au Rhum

With this recipe even a cake mix can fool many into thinking they are eating the real thing, which is a yeast-base cake, much more difficult to make. Make the day before — garnish with cream the day of the party — keep refrigerated.

The cream can be replaced by ice cream, or, both can be omitted and the cake served flambé with more rum.

> **1 box yellow cake mix of your choice**
> **½ cup sugar**
> **½ cup water**
> **½ cup dark rum**
> **1 cup whipping cream**
> **3 tbsp. icing sugar**
> **2 tbsp. dark rum**

Butter an 8-inch ring mold pan very thoroughly, then sprinkle with sugar and shake pan to remove excess. Mix the cake according to package directions. Pour enough of the batter into the prepared mold to reach to a little more than half way up the mold. Bake in a preheated oven for 25 to 30 minutes or until a toothpick inserted in the cake comes out with no batter clinging to it. Let stand on cake rack for 10 minutes before unmolding.

While cake is baking, combine the sugar with the water, and stir over medium heat until sugar has dissolved. Remove from heat and stir in the rum. Unmold the cake on to a service plate and pour the hot syrup over the hot cake: it will soak in immediately. If any syrup remains on the plate, spoon it gradually on the cake. Do not refrigerate, even overnight.

To serve, fill centre of ring with the cream, whipped and flavored with the sugar and rum. Garnish cream with rose petals or candied violets.

My Favorite Brunch

Surprise Tomato Juice or
Sliced Oranges in the Pink
Cheese Omelette Baveuse
Bouquets of Crisp Watercress
Paper-Thin Slices of Cold Ham
Toasted French Bread, unsalted butter
English Muffins
Homemade Currant Jam
Earl Grey Tea

Surprise Tomato Juice

Peel 1 medium-sized cucumber and grate finely, removing the seeds as they accumulate on the grater. Add to 5 or 6 cups of tomato juice with 1 tsp. of sugar, salt, and pepper to taste. Refrigerate a few hours or overnight.

When ready to serve, add the juice of ½ a lemon, or 1 tbsp. of Worcestershire sauce or ½ cup of dry gin or vodka. Serve strained or unstrained over ice cubes in cocktail glasses.

Sliced Oranges in the Pink

Peel 6 or 7 oranges and slice as thinly as possible. Place them in a cut-glass dish. Thaw a box of sliced, sweetened strawberries; pour over the oranges but do not mix. Cover and leave overnight at room temperature. Stir just before serving.

Cheese Omelette Baveuse

This is the French type of creamy omelette — an easy and successful way to make a light 6-egg omelette.

6 eggs
6 tbsp. cold water or milk
3 tbsp. butter
½ cup Swiss or mild cheddar cheese, grated
2 tbsp. Parmesan cheese, grated
1 tbsp. parsley, minced

Beat the eggs with the water; salt and pepper to taste. Melt the butter over high heat in a teflon-lined frying pan. Pour in the eggs, but do not stir. Lift the pan off the heat slightly and tilt it so that the egg mixture will run to one side and set in a thin film. Lift up this film with a wooden or nylon spatula and let more of the mixture run under it. Keep tilting, first to one side and then to the other, until most of the mixture is set. Some will still be soft in the middle.

Sprinkle the mixed cheeses on top of the omelette, fold, and slide it out of the pan on to a hot serving platter. Sprinkle with the parsley and serve with a bowl of watercress. The grated cheese will melt sufficiently while the omelette is being served. Serves 4 to 6.

English Muffins

An English muffin should always be *torn* apart before toasting. At home it is difficult to have muffins that look like the commercial type, all the same size and shape. These may be irregular here and there, but how good they are!

1 envelope active dry yeast
½ cup hot water (about 110°F.)
1 tsp. sugar
1 cup hot tap water
3 tbsp. butter, at room temperature
1½ tbsp. sugar
1 tsp. salt
½ cup non-fat dry milk
4½ to 5½ cups all-purpose flour
1 egg
cornmeal

In a cup, stir together the first three ingredients. Let stand 10 minutes. Mix the next five ingredients with 3 cups of flour in a large mixing bowl until well blended, then add the yeast mixture. Beat at medium speed in an electric mixer for 2 minutes (3 minutes by hand). Then beat in the egg and mix well.

Begin to add the remaining flour ¼ cup at a time, until the dough is a rough mass that cleans the side of the bowl. Keep at least ½ cup of the flour for the board, or work surface. Turn dough on to this flour and knead by hand for 5 to 8 minutes. (If your mixer has a dough hook, beat 6 minutes.)

Then turn dough into an oiled bowl. Cover with plastic wrap or a tea towel and let rise in a warm place until double in size (about 1 hr.).

Then punch down and knead in bowl for 30 seconds; let it rest for 10 minutes. Sprinkle the work surface with meal — a few spoonfuls should suffice. Turn dough on to it and roll out until ¼-inch thick. If dough resists the rolling pin and pulls back, let it rest 2 minutes, then resume rolling. Finally, cut into 3-inch rounds. Sprinkle rounds on both sides with more cornmeal and place on table next to each other. Cover with towel and let them rest and rise until they are about ½-inch thick, 15 to 20 minutes.

To cook: Heat a heavy griddle, pancake pan or a large cast iron frying pan. The heat is right when a piece of newspaper placed in the middle of the pan turns brown. With a spatula, place muffins gently on the griddle, leaving space between. Cook two minutes on each side, turning with spatula. Reduce heat to quite low, and cook an additional 5 to 6 minutes per side. If they scorch, it is because the heat is too high. With an electric stove, it is a good idea to remove the pan from the heat for 1 minute after cooking for two minutes on each side. Count the cooking time as if the pan were still on the heat.

Cool on a metal cake rack. To toast, pull apart with the tines of a fork or the fingers. These muffins will keep 3 to 4 months in the freezer. *Yield:* About 24 muffins.

Fritters can be made with fruit, vegetables, and even meat — calorie-laden, but so delicious. Recipe on page 73.

An Easy Weekend with Guests

16

People change when they become guests. At home they can live on a steady diet of sameness, but when they visit, they tend to eat more, drink more, and sleep more. With this in mind, here are my rules for enjoyable weekends.

Meals should be planned ahead and so designed that half your work is done before the weekend.

The dangerous time in a weekend is the hour before dinner. I am sure that, like me, you have often sat in someone's living room, watching the clock crawl and conversation fade. A cool beer, a dry martini, a fresh sherry, or a gay hostess (not strained by kitchen worry) can make this hour happy.

Guests sleep more, so why can't you? You can have your morning to yourself if you tell your female guests you will serve them a delicious brunch on Saturday or Sunday. Rarely will you get an objection from them and you will find that fixing a breakfast tray is easier than setting the table for many. As for the male guest, his normal habits will probably prevail, so have a tray ready for him in the kitchen and let him rise as early as he wants for fishing or golfing.

Guest rooms must have ashtrays, matches, cigarettes (if you like), a few interesting magazines or books (a must), a bouquet of flowers, a good bed, and emergency blankets for cool nights.

Do not make three big meals a day. On most weekends, I make only a big evening meal. I leave fruit, milk, cake, or cookies within easy reach for the midnight refrigerator raiders — with cups and glasses, spoons, knives, and attractive paper napkins handy on a tray.

To simplify my marketing, I prepare my weekend menu and make a complete list of all I need way ahead of time. I pin the menu in the kitchen for easy reference.

Plan some activities that you can enjoy together; others that you can do separately.

Friday Welcome Snacks

Your guests arrive Friday after dinner. When they are settled, a drink and a light snack will start off their visit with you on the right note.

Viva Italia

Serve a ready-made pizza, cut into small wedges — each wedge topped with a smoked sardine, hidden under a slice of cheese, and the whole sprinkled with basil or marjoram. Heat in 350°F. oven. Use attractive paper napkins and a round, shallow basket to hold the aluminum plate the ready pizza comes in. It saves washing plates and a platter. When finished, throw out the aluminum plate and napkins; hang up the basket. Perfect with cold beer.

Summer Gala

Make your entrance with fresh peaches in champagne, or sparkling wine, or port wine, or vin rosé. To munch with this, offer lovely light biscuits such as: doigts de dame, champagne fingers, or little langues de chats. Look for them in the fancy biscuit shelves of gourmet shops.

Oh yes, the peaches! Peel and slice them thinly, sugar ever so lightly, place in a covered glass jar, and refrigerate until ready to serve. Then transfer a fair portion of the peaches to a cold champagne glass or old-fashioned glass, and fill the glass with the chosen wine. If you like, top with a rose petal or a violet.

Saturday Lunch

If you plan to take your guests out to lunch, I have one suggestion: choose an interesting restaurant beforehand, making reservations, and, order lunch for all. This will give your guests a feeling of really being looked after.

If you plan lunch at home, make it light, buffet style. And why not serve it in the kitchen, as I often do? This should be the one effortless meal of the weekend. So, follow a menu in which there will be no cooking — or just the minimum. Have everything in the refrigerator, ready to serve. My kitchen buffet lunches are always fun. I try to serve them with a flourish — usually displaying the menu on a blackboard hanging over the table.

Ring-Around-the-Rosy
Snow in the Summer
Tipsy Seventh Cloud Cake

Ring-Around-the-Rosy

On Friday morning, boil (separately) some beets, unpeeled potatoes, and young carrots. When cooked, peel and slice them. Place in separate bowls. Blend each one with your favorite French dressing. Cover and refrigerate. Mince an equal quantity of parsley and celery leaves; mix and place in a covered glass container.

After breakfast on Saturday, take all of it out of the refrigerator. Choose a colorful meat platter, fill the middle with attractive dollops of carrots, beets, and potatoes. Surround with boiled eggs, rolled first in mayonnaise, then in the parsley and celery leaf mixture, until they look like green eggs. Place around the vegetable posy. Cover and refrigerate until lunch.

Snow in the Summer

Late Friday afternoon, grind very fine 4 tbsp. blanched almonds or walnuts. Add 2 tbsp. rose-water, grated peel of 1 orange, ½ cup white wine, nutmeg to taste, and a pinch of rosemary. Pour ½ pint whipping cream over the whole. Blend very well. Cover and refrigerate until you are ready to serve. Strain and add fruit sugar to taste (about 2 to 3 tbsp. is about right) and whip until frothy. Pour into a glass dish — it will look like snow. Keep refrigerated until serving time.

Tipsy Seventh Cloud Cake

Buy a white angel-food cake or make one on Thursday or Friday from your favorite cake mix (they keep very well). When you whip your Snow in the Summer, take the same white wine and saturate the cake with at least 1 cup of it. Sprinkle with instant cocoa. To serve, break off a piece with two forks and top with Snow in the Summer.

Saturday Dinner

Come sundown, cast a magic spell with a romantic candlelight supper. Of course, all the children are in bed, even if it means eating at 9:30 p.m. — who cares in the summer? Oh yes, the children have to be fed first: why not send them into the garden or the terrace or the balcony with a picnic box? Let them enjoy themselves — maybe even fight a bit. Come 7 or 8 p.m., they will be ready for bed. Then you can see to the finishing touches of your dinner — try to fix it so that you can enjoy a tall, cool drink with the others. Here is one of those dinners you may make, as I have, happily ever after.

Iced Soup Rosée Héloïse
Coq au Vin
Rice Paprika
Potted French Garden Peas
Authentic English Trifle

Iced Soup Rosée Héloïse

Peel 2 lbs. fresh tomatoes by first pouring boiling water over them. Cut them in half and press through a metal sieve to extract as much juice and pulp as possible. Add juice of 1 orange and half a lemon, 1 wine glass white wine, and 1 tsp. sugar, plus salt and pepper. Blend together well. Refrigerate 6 to 8 hours, or more, if you wish. Pour from a glass jug into champagne glasses with an ice cube in each glass. If you have the time and the inclination, make frozen flower ice cubes by placing a small fresh flower in each square of the ice tray, fill with boiled, cooled water, and freeze. Nasturtiums, borage, or violets are very pretty. Place flower cubes in glasses set on a tray and pour the soup individually for each guest.

Coq au Vin

Remove fat from a 4 to 4½ lb. boiling fowl. Melt fat in large saucepan. Cut fowl into individual pieces, brown all over in fat. Remove pieces to a plate. In their place put 8 small peeled onions and 8 small whole carrots. Sprinkle with ½ tsp. sugar and brown very lightly. Add 1 clove crushed garlic and stir in 3 tbsp. flour. Blend well. Gradually add 2 cups dry red wine, 1 small bay leaf, ¼ tsp. thyme, and savory. Bring to boil, stirring all the time. Then add 1 small can button mushrooms with liquid. Place chicken pieces into this sauce. Cover and cook for 2 to 3 hours over low heat. Just simmer; do not boil. When chicken is tender, it is ready. Remember, dishes cooked with wine are better if allowed to get cold, then reheated.

Rice Paprika

Boil 1 lb. rice according to directions on package. Mix together 4 tbsp. butter and 1 tbsp. paprika. Blend in cooked rice with a fork, until each grain is coated with the red butter. Serve garnished with a ring of parsley around the dish.

Potted Fresh Garden Peas

Shell 2 to 3 lbs. fresh green peas. Place in glass canning jar. Add ½ tsp. sugar, 1 tbsp. butter, a few sprigs of fresh mint. Cover. To cook, place jar in cold water in high saucepan like the bottom of a double boiler. Bring water to a boil, cover saucepan, and simmer for 1 hour. Do not open jar until ready to serve, just leave in hot water. Do not salt, pepper, or drain the peas.

Authentic English Trifle

First, make a soft rich custard. Beat 4 egg yolks until light and pale yellow. Heat 2 cups light cream with ¼ cup sugar and 1 tbsp. orange flower water or vanilla. Add beaten egg yolks, while beating very hard. Then cook without boiling, stirring continuously until custard coats the spoon. Remove to a bowl. Cover and refrigerate until well chilled.

Cut a two-layer sponge cake (that you bake or buy) into finger-length pieces. Spread each one on one side with raspberry jam and quickly dip in ½ cup sherry. Place half these sponge fingers in the bottom of a deep cut-glass bowl. Cover with half the custard. Whip 2 cups cream, sweeten with ½ cup icing sugar and vanilla to taste. Cover custard with half the whipped cream. Make a second layer on top of all this. Top with a dozen or so toasted almonds, standing them upright in the cream, and a few slivers of angelica, or use small roses instead of almonds and angelica. Refrigerate for at least 12 hours.

This beautiful dessert never fails to create a sensation, yet it is so easy to prepare.

On Sunday, Sleep In

When you go to bed Saturday night, you will not be in a hurry to get back into your apron again. So do as the others do (your guests and your husband). Sleep in Sunday to your heart's content. If you have a little girl, who is sweet and nice, and old enough to take care of breakfast, then of course you can. But there is another way!

Let the early risers look after themselves. Have instant coffee, fruit, buns, or doughnuts ready. Show them the night before where things are. Then sleep in peace on Sunday morning.

And now, what about the other Sunday meals? Because most weekend guests leave early in the afternoon, a good brunch served late is ideal. Here again you should have only one dish to cook at the last minute. My most popular brunch has everything, except the eggs, cooked or prepared right at the table. The menu is:

Canteloupe
Whipped Cream Chicken Livers, or, Eggs Bercy
Bread or buns with jam, jelly, or marmalade
Coffee

Do not reject the Whipped Cream Chicken Livers. They are delicious, and you will find you can never make enough. The alternative, Eggs Bercy, is down-to-earth baked eggs with sausages and tomato sauce.

Whipped Cream Chicken Livers
So rich, but so good!

Clean 1 lb. (about 15) chicken livers, roll in flour. Melt 4 tbsp. butter in electric frying pan. Raise the heat and brown livers quickly. Add salt, pepper, tarragon, or basil, to taste. Have a plateful of toast triangles, unbuttered. In a bowl, pour 1 cup whipped sour or fresh cream and mix with 1 tbsp. onion, ½ tsp. salt. Place about ⅓ cup of the cream on each warmed plate, and fill centre with cooked livers. Garnish with toast points. Serve with pride.

Be creative: Replace chicken liver with diced calves liver or diced blanched sweetbreads. Add a little sherry or a sprinkling of nutmeg instead of tarragon or basil. Replace whipped cream with a cheese or mushroom sauce, or freshly cooked asparagus, and remember, the whole can be cooked right at the brunch table in the modern chafing dish: the electric frying pan.

Eggs Bercy
Melt some butter. For each portion, put 1 tsp. of melted butter in bottom of an individual dish or custard cup. Carefully break in an egg and spoon a little melted butter on top. Prepare as far ahead as you wish, but remember, the eggs take 15 minutes to cook in a 350°F. oven. So time yourself accordingly. While they are cooking, pan fry cocktail sausages or large ones cut into three pieces. When almost done, sprinkle with a pinch of marjoram — the aroma will delight everyone. Have a bowl of hot tomato sauce, or chili sauce warmed up with a bit of curry powder with sherry. To serve, place a few sausages over the cooked egg, sprinkle with minced chives or parsley, and let each person help himself to the sauce.

Be creative: Put a thin slice of cheese in bottom of dish, break egg on top, bake the same way. Or, quickly pass in hot butter, some fresh, thinly sliced mushrooms, put in bottom of dish, finish as above. Or, sprinkle cooked egg with minced fresh basil, or diced, crisp bacon. Or, simmer sausages for 5 minutes in a bit of beer, then brown. Or, simmer sausages 5 minutes in apple juice. Drain, wrap each one in a slice of bacon. Fry. Or, replace the tomato sauce with broiled half tomatoes, sprinkled with basil.

Basic French Cooking Techniques

17

Gastronomy has long been the privilege of France, and still is. Try a few of the following basic French cooking techniques and notice what a difference they make to your favorite recipes.

Meatless Fond Brun

This basic sauce is easy to make, not expensive, and will keep 2 to 3 weeks refrigerated, 6 months frozen. Even only a few spoonfuls added to any sauce gives it that French flavor.

2 tbsp. butter or salad oil
the raw bones from 2 chicken breasts
2 cloves garlic, cut into four
1 cup diced onions
3/4 cup diced celery
3/4 cup diced carrots
1 tsp. thyme
2 bay leaves
1 tsp. salt
1/2 tsp. peppercorns
6 sprigs parsley (optional)
3 tbsp. flour
3 cups water

Heat the butter or salad oil in saucepan. Crush the bones (all meat removed) with a wooden mallet (it is easy, as they do not have to be fine, just broken up). Add to the hot fat, and stir over high heat until the whole takes on a caramel color.

Add the onions, carrots, celery, thyme, bay leaves, salt, and peppercorns. Stir together, still over high heat, about 3 to 4 minutes, but do not let it burn. Add the flour, stir until mixed, then add the water. Bring back to boil while stirring. Cover and simmer, over low heat for 1½ hours. Stir 2 to 3 times during that period. Strain through a fine colander or one lined with cheesecloth. When cool, pour into a container, cover, and refrigerate. Yield: 3 cups sauce.

French Salt

Keep this salt handy in your spice rack; use it whenever you wish a subtle flavor of herbs. It keeps for months in a tightly closed container.

1 tbsp. broken bay leaves
1 tbsp. dried thyme
1 tbsp. powdered mace
1 tbsp. dried basil
1 tsp. dried rosemary
2 tbsp. cinnamon
1/2 tbsp. ground cloves
1/2 tsp. ground nutmeg
1/2 tsp. ground allspice
1 tsp. freshly ground pepper
2 tsp. paprika
1 cup salt

Place everything in a mortar or a bowl and pound and push until the whole is well blended. Sift through a sieve, crush again what is left in the sieve. Pour into tightly closed container.

Browning Oil for Meat

Use this oil to brush the whole surface of any meat or poultry. The result is marvellous, giving a caramel color to the food, while flavoring it. A must in any kitchen.

- ½ cup olive or peanut oil
- ½ cup Kitchen Bouquet
- 1 clove garlic, cut in half
- 2 bay leaves

Mix and keep in a bottle. It does not need refrigeration; just keep it at room temperature, well corked.

Double Consommé the Easy Way

The classic recipe is costly, involved, and honestly does not taste better than this one.

- 4 cans (10½ oz. each) beef consommé, undiluted
- 4 cans cold water
- 1 lb. lean ground beef
- 2 egg whites
- 1 carrot, finely grated
- 1 bay leaf
- ¼ tsp. thyme
- 1 tbsp. unsalted butter
- 1 tsp. cornstarch
- 1 cup cold water
- dry sherry or dry Madeira, to taste

Pour the consommé and the 4 cans of cold water in a saucepan.

Beat the egg whites and blend thoroughly with the meat. Add slowly to the cold consommé, beating well after each addition, so that all meat particles separate. Place the carrot, bay leaf, and thyme in the melted butter; stir over low heat until carrot is coated with the butter. Add to consommé mixture.

Mix the cornstarch with the cup of cold water. Set aside.

Bring the soup to boil, over medium heat, beating with a whisk every 4 to 5 minutes. When the soup is boiling rapidly, remove from heat. Add cornstarch and cold water mixture while stirring. Bring back to boil, still stirring. Then cover, and simmer over very low heat for 1 hour. Turn off the heat and let stand for another hour.

To use the same day, the fat must be skimmed, or else refrigerated. Remove fat hardened on top, warm up, then pass through a strainer lined with cheesecloth. Let it drip naturally, without touching.

To serve, reheat, but do not boil. Add wine to taste.

The leftover meat and carrots can be used to make a shepherd's pie. To keep the consommé for a week to 10 days, strain while hot, pour into a container, cover, and refrigerate. The fat layer that will rise and harden on top will keep the consommé fresh. Yield: 8 to 9 cups.

Easy Clarified Butter

This butter will keep for months refrigerated, well covered. Use it to fry delicate foods over high heat as it will brown, but not burn.

- ½ lb. unsalted butter

Place the cut-up butter in a Pyrex 2-cup size measuring cup. Place in a 250°F. oven until the butter has melted. It should take from 10 to 20 minutes, depending on the temperature of the butter.

Carefully skim the foam off the top of the butter and pour into a container (with a good cover) the clarified butter off the top, without using any of the milky residue in the bottom of the cup. (Do not throw it away, use in white sauce or cream soups.) Yield: ¾ cup, as clarified butter loses one quarter of its original volume.

Beurre Manié

Keep handy in covered glass jar, refrigerated. Then in no time you can cream or thicken all types of sauces, gravies, soups, and stews. The fresh lemon juice prevents spoilage.

- 1 cup butter, at room temperature
- 1 cup flour
- 1 tbsp. fresh lemon juice
- ⅛ tsp. nutmeg or thyme (optional)

Beat together until creamy. Place in container and refrigerate. To add to sauce, whisk a teaspoon at a time into hot liquid. Let simmer a few seconds; keep adding until you get the desired consistency.

How to Correct Mistakes

18

You are not paying attention and you have burned the stew or overcooked the cabbage. Or, you want to thicken a sauce and there is not a speck of flour or cornstarch in the house. What to do? Solutions to these and other problems follow, but also included are hints on how to avoid making mistakes. The well-organized Chinese cook who has everything washed, cut, trimmed, measured, and on hand before he begins is the example we should all try to follow. Prevention means taking the time to get ready before you start cooking.

Eggs

Eggs are not as uncomplicated as they seem — a lot can go wrong with them. Store them the same way they're packaged (with the small point down, which keeps the yolk in the middle) and never add salt while they're cooking. Add it only when they're served; otherwise salt will toughen them.

Hard-boiled eggs: If yours come out with the yolk along one side instead of neatly in the middle, you are probably cooking them in too small a pan. Put them in lots of cold (not boiling) water in a pan with plenty of space.

Eggs sticking to carton: Simply set the carton in a pan of cold water for a few minutes. Keep these eggs refrigerated in a bowl and use as soon as possible in case the moisture has affected them.

Yolk in egg whites: The least bit will prevent beaten whites from stiffening properly. You can use a piece of broken shell to pick up the yolk, but the chef's way is best — moisten a corner of a cloth in cold water and just touch the yolk with it. The yolk will cling as if to a magnet.

Volume in egg whites: They will increase more in size if they are at room temperature before being beaten. You can use an ordinary wire whisk, a hand rotary beater, or an electric mixer, but for high volume and perfect texture, nothing can replace hand beating with the big double balloon wire whisk made especially for whipping cream or egg whites.

Egg yolk as thickener: Like flour and cornstarch, egg yolks can be used as a thickening agent for sauces, custards, and cream soups. Two yolks equal 1 tbsp. of flour. They must be cooked over very gentle heat. Stir 1 tbsp. of cold liquid or hot sauce into the yolks before you add them and stir constantly until the texture is velvety and creamy. Never let the sauce boil.

Overcooked scrambled eggs: You cannot rescue them, but you can use them. Keep cooking until they have dried up, cool, then chop to use over lettuce or canned salmon, or to mix with diced celery and mayonnaise for an egg salad.

Sugar

To brown pot roast meat beautifully, use this chef's trick: Add 1 tbsp. of sugar to a few table-spoons of heated fat and cook over medium heat until sugar browns lightly. Add meat and brown on all sides; the sugar will give it a delectable flavor as well as color.

Hard lumpy sugar: Steam it in the top of a double boiler, then crush it with a spoon, spread it on a tray and cool. Or, put the sugar in a brown paper bag, close tightly and set in a 350°F. oven. When the bag is warm, the sugar should be soft enough to de-lump — just pass a rolling pin over the bag, then spread the sugar to cool.

Cooking vegetables: Add a pinch of sugar to the cooking water to bring out their finest flavor. Add salt only when serving.

Equivalents: One pound of icing sugar equals 3½ cups, sifted, 1 lb. of brown sugar equals 2¼ cups, firmly packed; and 1 lb. granulated sugar equals 2 cups.

Salt

It pays to be cautious when using salt; it is difficult to subtract from a dish, but it can always be added. It should be added to eggs or vegetables only after they have been cooked. Remember too that any simmering liquid becomes saltier as it cooks. Beef and chicken stocks should be salted lightly because the stock must be reduced for the best flavor and this concentrates the salt flavor as well.

Too salty sauce or soup: It can sometimes be brought back to normal by simmering an unpeeled potato, washed and quartered, in the liquid for 15 minutes. Discard the potato, add a pinch of sugar, stir, and taste.

Too salty potatoes: Drain off the cooking water and pour fresh boiling water over them. Stir a few seconds and drain again. This will usually remove enough of the salt to make them palatable.

Cabbage

Because cabbage needs very little cooking, it is easy to overdo the job and difficult to remedy. You can add diluted canned consommé and grated cheese to make a soup, or, cover the cabbage with a thick white sauce and grated cheese (cheese will always take away most of its strong taste), or, add the cabbage to mashed potatoes.

Potatoes

In late winter, before the new potatoes are available, they sometimes develop black spots when they are cooked. This happens because the frost has got to them. The next time you use potatoes from the same bag, start cooking them in cold water to which you have added 1 tsp. of vinegar or 2 slices of unpeeled lemon and boil them uncovered.

Stew

You have burned it. Immediately, put 5 or 6 ice cubes in another pot, pour contents of burned pot (without scraping bottom) over them and simmer on low heat until sauce is hot. The smell and taste of burning will be gone (and all you have left to do is clean the original pot).

Liver

To tenderize it and to prevent dryness, soak liver 1 to 4 hours in enough milk to cover. Drain, roll in flour, and fry over medium heat in butter or oil. Chicken livers will not splatter during cooking if you perforate them all over with a fork before you start.

Grapefruit

If you have a hard time removing the white skin, first boil the grapefruit for 5 minutes in enough water to cover. Cool, then peel — all the white skin should come away too. Or, just pour boiling water over grapefruit, let stand 5 minutes, then peel. Try grapefruit juice in place of vinegar in an oil and vinegar dressing — it's a pleasant change.

Lettuce

Do not cut out the core or remove the leaves with a knife — that's what causes rust. Twist the core to remove and pluck off the leaves. To store, place a few paper towels in the bottom of a plastic bag in which you have punched 4 or 5 holes. Clean lettuce before adding to bag — the paper will absorb the excess moisture.

Parsley

Even if it is a bit limp when you buy it you can revive it. Wash in cold water, shake well, and refrigerate in a covered glass jar. It will keep crisp and green for 4 to 5 days.

Olives and Pickles

When you have used the first few olives or pickles, float a teaspoon of salad oil on top of the liquid in the jar, cover, and refrigerate — they will keep for a year. The oil forms an airtight cover so no scum can form, but it will not mix with the pickle juices.

Tea

If, come summer, your iced tea gets cloudy, add a spoonful of boiling water to each glass. For making large quantities of tea, see the section on nylon net (below).

Odds and Ends

Refrigerators and Deep Freezers: To keep them smelling sweet, put a lump of charcoal in them. I put mine in a plastic ice cream container through which I have punched air holes with an ice pick. If food has already spoiled, place a pan of uncompressed charcoal in the main part of the refrigerator or freezer. Put fresh charcoal in the next day and leave the first out in the sun to dry for use the third day. The charcoal will gradually absorb the odors.

Glasses: When two are stuck together, put cold water in the top glass and place the bottom in hot water. They will come apart easily after a few seconds.

Nylon Net: Learn how useful this can be in the kitchen. When a recipe calls for straining through a fine strainer or cheesecloth, nylon net not only works beautifully, it is easy to rinse, dry, and reuse. Net also is handy for making giant-size tea bags if you're making large quantities for a party. Fold in several thicknesses, add quantity of tea required, and tie with a string. The bag can be reused many times.

How to Adapt to Metric Measures

19

The 250 ml measure replaces the 8 oz. cup, which involves a 5% increase in amounts. Certain cooking items, such as eggs and possibly gelatine and cooking chocolate will not increase. The ¼, ¾, ⅓, and ⅔ divisions of 1 cup do not convert to multiples of 25, so these quantities require rounding up or down. Other replacements are:

15 ml for a tablespoon
5 ml for a teaspoon
5 cm is about 2 inches
1 kg is a little more than 2 pounds
500 g is a little more than 1 pound
100°C water boils
160°C oven temperature for roasting
185°C temperature for deep fat frying

60°C internal temperature of rare roast beef
65°C internal temperature of medium roast beef
75°C internal temperature of well done beef
80°C internal temperature of cooked fresh pork
85°C internal temperature of cooked poultry

Conversion tables are not required. Their use only confuses and complicates learning the metric cooking system. For best results, proceed carefully and use common sense — as you acquire experience in preparing these recipes with metric weights, measures, and temperatures, you will be able to gauge visually the correct proportions.

The above adaptations are courtesy of The Metric Committee, Canadian Home Economics Association, Ottawa, Canada.

Index

Photo Credits

Tim Saunders on pages 17, 71, 89.

Karol Ike on pages 18, 53, 54.

Gillian Proctor on page 35.

Phillip Gallard on pages 36, 90, 107.